GED® TEST

FLASH REVIEW

GED® TEST
FLASH REVIEW

NEW YORK

Printed in the United States of America

9 8 7 6 5 4 3 2 1

First Edition

ISBN 978-1-57685-9254

For more information or to place an order, contact
LearningExpress at:
    80 Broad Street
    Suite 400
    New York, NY 10004

Or visit us at:
    www.learningexpressllc.com

CONTENTS

GED® TEST

FLASH REVIEW

INTRODUCTION

About the GED® Test

The GED® test is a series of five examinations, created by the GED® Testing Service, that are designed to measure your proficiency in high school-level curriculum. The tests include Language Arts, Writing; Language Arts, Reading; Social Studies; Science; and Mathematics. Students are expected to have a solid grasp of these core subject areas and be able to analyze information provided, problem solve, and communicate their thoughts and ideas appropriately.

The GED® tests, which include a direct writing assessment, take more than seven hours to complete. Students who pass the GED® tests receive certification that is equivalent to a high school diploma.

The GED® tests are available to students who meet the necessary state requirements— please contact the official GED® Testing Service (www.gedtestingservice.com/ged-testing-service) for requirements, application and registration information, and locations of GED® test centers near you.

How the GED® Tests are Scored

Each GED® test is scored within a range of 200 to 800, and students earning a minimum score of 410 on each test and a minimum average test score of 450 are awarded with a GED® test credential.

GED® Test Overview

The following is a breakdown of the major topic areas covered on each GED® test subtest:

Language Arts, Reading

40 multiple-choice questions that cover the following:

- Fictional literature (75% of test), including at least one selection from each of the following:

- Poetry
- Drama
- Prose fiction before 1920
- Prose fiction between 1920 and 1960
- Prose fiction after 1960
- Nonfiction (25% of test), including two selections of nonfiction prose from any two of the following areas:
  - Nonfiction prose
  - Visual and performing arts reviews
  - Workplace and community documents

Language Arts, Writing

The Language Arts, Writing content area is divided into two parts (scores are combined and reported as one score).

Part I

50 multiple-choice questions covering the following content areas:

- Organization (15%)
- Sentence structure (30%)

- Usage (30%)
- Mechanics (25%)

Part II

This part of the test requires you to write an essay on a familiar subject. You'll have 45 minutes to plan, write, and edit your essay. You'll be required to present your opinion or explain your views on a provided topic, and your essay will be scored on the following:

- Focused main points
- Clear organization
- Specific development of ideas
- Sentence structure control, punctuation, grammar, word choice, and spelling

Each essay reader will score your work on a four-point scale, and your scores will be averaged to make up your final score. If you earn a final score of less than two, you must retake the Language Arts, Writing exam.

Mathematics

50 questions (80% multiple-choice questions; 20% constructed answers) divided into two parts, focusing on the following:

- Number operations and number sense (20–30%)
- Measurement and geometry (20–30%)
- Data analysis, statistics, and probability (20–30%)
- Algebra, functions, and patterns (20–30%)

In addition to multiple-choice questions, constructed answer questions will require you to write answers on either standard or coordinate plane grids.

Social Studies

50 multiple-choice questions from the following content areas:

- History (U.S. or Canada, 25%; World, 15%)
- Geography (15%)

- Civics and government (25%)
- Economics (20%)

Science

50 multiple-choice questions from the following content areas:

- Physical science (physics and chemistry, 35%)
- Life science (45%)
- Earth and space science (20%)

Information on each GED® test subtest is available on the official GED® test website: www .gedtestingservice.com/ged-testing-service.

How to Use this Book

GED® Test Flash Review is designed to help you prepare for and succeed on each of the subtests that make up the GED® test. It contains 600 of the most commonly covered terms on the exam, along with their definitions, for quick and effective study and review. On one side of the page are three essential GED® test terms; on the reverse side are their definitions and/or explanations. The terms are alphabetized for easy access.

Please note that this book is not designed to give an exhaustive review of the entire scope of the concepts covered inside; it is meant to give you a concise, general overview of concepts that you will likely need to know in order to succeed on the GED® test. Being fully aware of the essential terms covered in this book will put you in a great position for GED® test success.

Using this Book to Prepare for the GED® Test

The following are some suggestions for making the most of *GED® Test Flash Review* as you structure your study plan:

- Do not try to learn or memorize all of the 600 terms covered in this book all at once. Cramming is not the most effective approach to test prep. The best approach is to build a realistic study schedule that lets you review around 10–15 terms each day. Review a set of terms and then quiz yourself to see how well you've learned them.

- Mark the terms that you have trouble with, so that they will be easy to return to later for further study.
- As you prepare for the GED® test, you may come across terms that are unfamiliar or difficult for you. We recommend that you consult this book for a quick review of the terms and concepts that often appear on the GED® test.
- Make the most of this book's portability—take it with you wherever and whenever you have some free study time.

A

ABOLITIONISM

. . . .

ABSOLUTE VALUE

. . . .

ABSTRACT LANGUAGE

A reform movement during the eighteenth and nineteenth centuries that advocated the end of African slavery in Europe and the Americas.

· ·

For a number, this is the distance, or number of units, from the origin on a number line. Absolute value is the size of the number and is always positive. For example, |−5| = 5

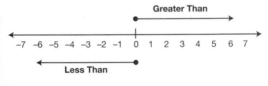

· ·

Words or phrases that refer to intangible ideas or to classes of people and objects rather than the people or things themselves. Abstractions are built on concrete ideas.

ACCELERATION

. . . .

ACCELERATION DUE TO GRAVITY

. . . .

ACCURACY

The rate that velocity changes per unit of time and the direction it changes in, computed from the change in velocity divided by the change in time.

$$a = \frac{\Delta V}{\Delta t} = \frac{V_f - V_i}{t_f - t_i}$$

Common units are meters per second squared (m/s^2).

. . . .

The acceleration of an object that is only acted on by the force of Earth's gravity. This value is given the symbol g, and near the surface of Earth, it has a value of approximately $9.8\ m/s^2$. The direction of acceleration due to gravity is downward.

. . . .

The closeness of an experimental measurement to the accepted or theoretical value.

ACID

. . . .

ACTIVE VOICE

. . . .

ACUTE ANGLE

A substance that is a proton donor. The pH of an acid is less than 7.

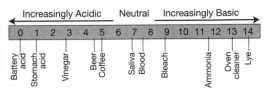

· ·

In an active sentence, the subject performs the action of the verb. The person or thing that performs the action is named before the verb, or the action word(s).

Examples:

James <u>filed</u> the papers yesterday.

Jin Lee <u>sang</u> the song beautifully.

· ·

An angle that measures less than 90°.

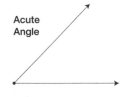

ADDEND

. . . .

ADJACENT ANGLE

. . . .

A number that is to be part of an addition process. *In 3 + 2 = 5, the three and the two are the addends.*

. . . .

Adjacent angles have the same vertex, share a side, and do not overlap.

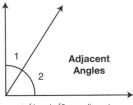

∠1 and ∠2 are adjacent.

. . . .

ADJECTIVE

. . . .

ADVERB

. . . .

A

A word that describes a noun or pronoun in a sentence. Adjectives answer one of three questions about another word in a sentence: Which one? What kind? How many?

Which one?	What kind?	How many?
that book	*romance* novel	*several* chapters
the *other* class	*steep* expense	*multiple* choices
the *last* song	*jazzy* melody	*six* awards

. . . .

A word that describes verbs, adjectives, and other adverbs. Adverbs answer one of these questions about another word in the sentence: Where? When? How? To what extent?

Where?	When?	How?	To What Extent?
The plane flew *south*.	Jude arrived *early*.	She sang *beautifully*.	Anthony is *very* talented.
Put the chair *here*.	She registered *late*.	The system is behaving *erratically*.	Eleanor is still *extremely* ill.

. . . .

ALLIED POWERS

. . . .

ALLITERATION

. . . .

A military coalition formed between nations in opposition to another alliance of countries. In World War I, the Allied Powers included 28 nations that opposed the Central Powers. In World War II, the Allied Powers fought the Axis Powers.

World War I European Powers

- -

The repetition of sounds, especially at the beginning of words. For example, "She sells seashells down by the seashore" and "Peter Piper picked a peck of pickled peppers" are both alliterative phrases.

- -

AMENDMENT

. . . .

ANALYSIS

. . . .

ANTAGONIST

A

A *change* or addition to a motion, bill, written basic law, or constitution. The U.S. Constitution has 27 amendments. The first ten are collectively known as the Bill of Rights.

. . . .

A stage in the scientific method where patterns of the observations are made.

. . . .

The person, force, or idea working against the protagonist.

ANTECEDENT

. . . .

ANTIBIOTIC

. . . .

ANTIHERO

A

The word or words to which a specific pronoun refers. In the sentence, "Denise lost an earring and she can't find it," *Denise* is the antecedent of the pronoun *she* and *earring* is the antecedent of the pronoun *it*.

. . . .

A compound or substance that kills bacteria without harming our own cells.

. . . .

A character who is pathetic rather than tragic, and who does not take responsibility for his or her destructive actions.

APOSTROPHE

....

APPOSITIVE

....

AQUEOUS SOLUTION

A

A symbol (') used to show possession; it shows to whom or what a noun belongs.

· ·

A word or group of words that immediately follows a noun or pronoun. The appositive makes the pronoun more defined by explaining or identifying it.

· ·

A solution in which the solvent is water.

ARCTIC ZONE

. . . .

AREA

. . . .

A

The climatic zone near the North and South Poles characterized by long, cold winters and short, cool summers.

. . . .

The inside shape or space of a two-dimensional figure, measured in square units. Formulas for finding the area of a:

Square: $A = side^2$
Rectangle: $A = length \times width$
Parallelogram: $A = base \times height$
Triangle: $A = \frac{1}{2}(base \times height)$
Trapezoid: $A = \frac{1}{2}(base_1 + base_2) \times height$
Circle: $A = \pi \times radius^2$; π is approximately equal to 3.14.

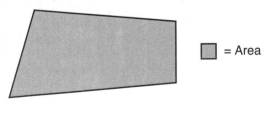

☐ = Area

. . . .

ARTERIES

. . . .

ARTICLES OF CONFEDERATION

. . . .

ASIDE

A

The vascular tissues that carry blood away from the heart.

. . . .

The first compact (agreement) uniting the American colonies; it was formally ratified by all 13 states in 1781. It was replaced by the U.S. Constitution in 1789.

. . . .

In drama, when a character speaks directly to the audience or another character concerning the action on stage, but only the audience or character addressed in the aside is meant to hear.

ASSOCIATIVE PROPERTY

. . . .

ASTRONOMY

. . . .

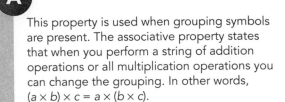

A

This property is used when grouping symbols are present. The associative property states that when you perform a string of addition operations or all multiplication operations you can change the grouping. In other words, $(a \times b) \times c = a \times (b \times c)$.

Example:
    $15 \times (8 \times 20) \times 5 =$

Change grouping to multiply 20 and 5 first, because $20 \times 5 = 100$: $15 \times 8 \times (20 \times 5)$. Evaluate parentheses first: $20 \times 5 = 100$. The problem becomes $15 \times 8 \times 100$. Finish, working left to right: $15 \times 8 = 120$, then $120 \times 100 = 12,000$.

· ·

The scientific study of celestial objects (stars, planets, comets, galaxies, etc.) and phenomena that originate outside the atmosphere of Earth. Astronomy is concerned with the positions, dimensions, distribution, composition, energy, evolution, and motion of celestial objects, as well as the formation and development of the universe.

· ·

ATOM

The smallest structure that has the properties of an element. Atoms contain positively charged protons and uncharged neutrons in the nucleus. Negatively charged electrons orbit around the nucleus.

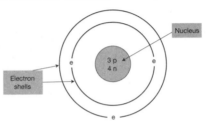

The figure above is a representation of a lithium atom (Li). It has 3 protons (p) and 4 neutrons (n) in the nucleus, and 3 electrons (e) in the two electron shells. Its atomic number is 3 (p). Its atomic mass is 7 amu (p + n). The atom has no net charge because the number of positively charged protons equals the number of negatively charged electrons.

Charges and Masses of Atomic Particles			
	Proton	Neutron	Electron
Charge	+1	0	−1
Mass	1 amu	1 amu	$\frac{1}{1,800}$ amu

ATP

. . . .

ATRIA

. . . .

AUTOBIOGRAPHY

A

Adenosine triphosphate (ATP) is a chemical that is considered to be the "fuel" or energy source for an organism.

. . . .

The chambers of the heart that receive blood.

. . . .

The true account of a person's life written by that person.

AXIS POWERS

. . . .

A

An alliance created between Germany, Italy, and Japan during World War II. The Axis Powers fought the Allied Powers.

. . . .

BALLAD

. . . .

BARTERING

. . . .

BASE (CHEMISTRY)

A poem that tells a story, usually rhyming. Typically, only the second and fourth lines of a quatrain are rhymed. It follows the rhyme scheme: *abcb defe ghih*, etc.

• •

As communities grew, a system of bartering—trading goods or services—developed.

• •

A substance that is a proton acceptor. The pH of a base is greater than 7.

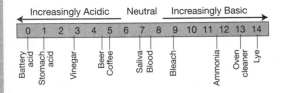

BASE (MATHEMATICS)

. . . .

BIG BANG THEORY

. . . .

A number used as a repeated factor in an exponential expression. In 8^5, 8 is the base number.

$2^5 \leftarrow$exponent $= 2 \times 2 \times 2 \times 2 \times 2 = 32$
$\uparrow$
base

. . . .

Nobody knows for sure how the universe originated. According to the Big Bang theory, the universe started off in a hot dense state under high pressure between 10 and 20 billion years ago. The Big Bang theory also postulates that the universe has been expanding since its origination.

. . . .

BILL OF RIGHTS

. . . .

BINARY SYSTEM

. . . .

B

The first ten amendments to the U.S. Constitution. Ratified in 1791, the Bill of Rights safeguards the liberties of individuals. These liberties include:

- the right to practice one's religion freely
- the right to free speech
- the right to a free press
- the right to bear firearms
- the right to meet and to petition the government
- the right to a fair and speedy trial
- the right to representation by a lawyer
- the right to know the crime with which one is being charged
- protection from being tried twice for the same crime
- protection from excessive bail and/or cruel and unusual punishment

. . . .

One of the simplest numbering systems. The base of the binary system is 2, which means that only the digits 0 and 1 can appear in a binary representation of any number.

. . . .

BISECT

. . . .

BLANK VERSE

. . . .

BOLSHEVIK

Cut in two equal parts.

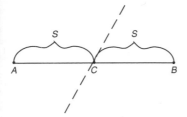

Line segment *AB* is bisected at point *C*.

. . . .

Poetry in which the structure is controlled only by a metrical scheme. Also called *metered verse*.

. . . .

A member of the radical faction of the Russian socialist party that took power in Russia and formed the Communist Party in 1918.

BOSTON TEA PARTY

. . . .

BRACKETS

. . . .

BUBONIC PLAGUE

B

A 1773 incident staged by American colonists protesting the British tax on tea. The colonists threw three shipments of tea into Boston Harbor.

· ·

Symbols ([ ]) used to close parenthetical material within parentheses, enclose words inserted into a quotation, and enclose the word *sic* to show that an error in quotation was made by the original writer or speaker.

· ·

An infectious disease that killed up to one-third of all Europeans in the fourteenth century. Also called "the Black Death."

BUSINESS CYCLE

. . . .

B

Periods of high and low productivity in a capitalist economy.

• •

CALIBRATION

. . . .

CAPILLARIES

. . . .

The examination of the performance of an instrument in an experiment whose outcomes are known, for the purpose of accounting for the inaccuracies inherent in the instrument in future experiments whose outcomes are not known.

· ·

Vascular tissues that receive blood from the arterioles and release the blood to the venuoles.

· ·

CAPITALISM

. . . .

An economic system in which individuals and private organizations produce and distribute goods and services in a free market.

Characteristics	Examples
• Individuals and private organizations own and operate businesses. • Free market determines production and distribution of goods and services. • Prices set by supply and demand.	• United States • Sweden • Australia

CATALYST

. . . .

CELESTIAL EQUATOR

. . . .

An agent that changes the rate of a reaction, without itself being altered by the reaction.

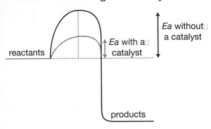

A catalyst acts by lowering the activation energy barrier (*Ea*) to product formation. In the diagram, the top hill represents a high activation energy. The catalyst acts to make the hill smaller, so that the bottom hill represents the activation energy in the presence of a catalyst.

. . . .

The extension of Earth's equator out onto the celestial sphere.

. . . .

CELESTIAL POLES

. . . .

CELESTIAL SPHERE

. . . .

C

The extension of Earth's North and South Poles onto the celestial sphere.

· ·

The imaginary sphere which all the stars are viewed as being on for the purposes of locating them.

· ·

CELL MEMBRANE

. . . .

CELL WALL

. . . .

C

An organelle found in all cells that acts as the passageway through which materials can pass in and out. The cell membrane is highly selectively permeable, only allowing materials to pass through that it "chooses" chemically. Also called the *plasma membrane*.

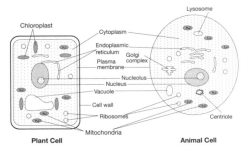

Plant Cell   **Animal Cell**

. . . .

An organelle found primarily in plant cells and fungi cells, and also some bacteria. The cell wall is a strong structure that provides protection and support, and allows materials to pass in and out without being selectively permeable.

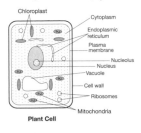

Plant Cell

. . . .

CENTRAL POWERS

. . . .

CENTRIPETAL FORCE

. . . .

A military coalition of nations that fought against the Allied Powers in World War I. The Central Powers included Austria-Hungary, Germany, Bulgaria, and Turkey.

World War I European Powers

. . . .

The net force that acts to result in centripetal acceleration. Centripetal force is not an individual force, but the sum of the forces in the radial direction. It is directed toward the center of the circular motion.

. . . .

CHARACTERS

. . . .

CHARTER

. . . .

CHECKS AND BALANCES

People created by an author to carry the action, language, and ideas of a story or play.

· ·

To approve or grant power to something, such as a town or city government.

· ·

A system outlined by the U.S. Constitution that divides authority between the executive, legislative, and judicial branches of the federal government so that no branch of government dominates the others.

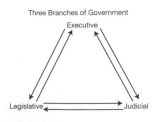

Three Branches of Government

CHEMICAL CHANGE

. . . .

CHORD

. . . .

A process that involves the formation or breaking of chemical bonds.

. . . .

A line segment that goes through a circle with its endpoints on the circle.

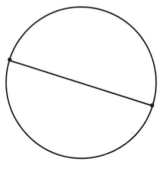

. . . .

CHROMOSOME

. . . .

CIRCLE

. . . .

C

An organized structure of DNA and protein found in cells.

. . . .

The set of all points equidistant from one given point, called the *center*. The center point defines the circle, but it is not on the circle.

. . . .

CIRCUMFERENCE

. . . .

CIVILIZATION

. . . .

C

The distance around the outside of a circle.
$C = \pi \times$ diameter; π is approximately equal
to 3.14.

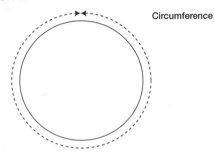

Circumference

Example:

Find the circumference of a circle with a
diameter of 5 inches.

Because you know the diameter, use the
formula that includes the diameter:

$C = \pi d$

$C = \pi(5)$

$\quad = (3.14)(5)$

$\quad = 15.7$

The final answer is 15.7 inches.

· ·

An advanced state of intellectual, cultural, and
technological development in human society.

· ·

CLAUSE

. . . .

CLICHÉ

. . . .

CLIMACTIC ZONE

C

A group of words that contains both a subject and a verb.

. . . .

A tired, overused word or phrase.

. . . .

Any of several broad areas that lie along latitudinal lines between the equator and the North and South Poles.

CLIMATE

. . . .

CLIMAX

. . . .

CLOSET DRAMA

C

The atmospheric characteristics near the earth's surface over a period of time. Climate includes average temperature, rainfall, humidity, wind, and barometric pressure.

. . . .

The turning point or high point of action and tension in the plot.

. . . .

A play that is meant only to be read, not performed.

COEFFICIENT

. . . .

COLD WAR

. . . .

COLLOQUIALISM

The number placed in front of a variable(s), such as 2 in the expression 2x.

· ·

Term for the post-World War II rivalry between the United States and the Union of Soviet Socialist Republics (USSR) that ended in 1989.

· ·

Informal word or phrase such as *a lot*, *in a bind*, *pulled it off*, and so on. These words are regularly used in conversations between friends, rather than in official written communication.

COLON

. . . .

COMEDY

. . . .

COMMA

Symbol (:) used to introduce a list of items, as long as the part before the colon is already a complete sentence.

· ·

Humorous writing or ideas.

· ·

Symbol (,) used to separate items in lists of similar words, phrases, or clauses to make the material easier for a reader to understand. Commas are often used before the final conjunction in a sentence.

COMMA SPLICE

....

COMMENSALISM

....

COMMENTARY

A type of run-on sentence in which a comma is used in place of a semicolon to join two independent clauses without a conjunction. Comma splices can be corrected by putting a semicolon in place of the comma or by adding a conjunction after the comma.

. . . .

A relationship between two organisms in which one organism benefits and the other is neither harmed nor rewarded. For example, barnacles are crustaceans that attach themselves to a hard surface, such as rocks, shells, whales, etc. When they attach to the shell of a scallop, for instance, barnacles benefit by having a place to stay, leaving the scallop unaffected.

. . . .

Literature written to explain or illuminate other works of literature or art.

COMMISSION

. . . .

COMMUNISM

. . . .

COMMUNIST MANIFESTO

C

A form of local government in which voters elect commissioners to head a city or county department, such as the fire, police, or public works department.

. . . .

An economic and political system in which the means of production are owned collectively and controlled by the state.

Characteristics	Examples
• State, or the community, owns *all* businesses. • State controls distribution of goods and services. • State provides social services.	• People's Republic of China • Cuba • Former Soviet Union

. . . .

A document of communist principles written by Karl Marx in 1848.

COMMUTATIVE PROPERTY

. . . .

COMPLEMENTARY ANGLES

. . . .

C

This property states that when performing a string of addition operations or a string of multiplication operations, the *order* does not matter. In other words, $a + b = b + a$.

Example:

$17 + 64 + 35 + 43 + 96 =$

Change the order: $17 + 43 + 64 + 96 + 35$.

Add 17 and 43 first, because $7 + 3 = 10$:

$17 + 43 = 60$.

The problem becomes $60 + 64 + 96 + 35$.

Add 64 and 96 next, because $4 + 6 = 10$:

$64 + 96 = 160$.

The problem becomes $60 + 160 + 35$.

Work left to right: $60 + 160 + 35 = 220 + 35 = 255$.

· ·

Two angles are complementary if the sum of their measures is equal to 90°.

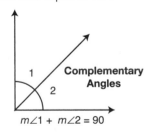

$m\angle 1 + m\angle 2 = 90$

· ·

COMPLETE SENTENCE

. . . .

COMPLICATION

. . . .

COMPONENT

C

A group of words that expresses a complete thought and has a verb and a subject. Also called an *independent clause*.

Independent clause: *She was excited.*

Dependent clause: *Because she was excited.*

Notice that the dependent clause is incomplete; it needs an additional thought to make a complete sentence, such as:

<u>She spoke very quickly</u> *because she was excited.*

The independent clause, however, can stand alone. It is a complete thought.

. . . .

The series of events that "complicate" the plot and build up to the climax.

. . . .

The part of a vector that lies in the horizontal or vertical direction.

COMPOSITE NUMBER

. . . .

COMPOUND

. . . .

CONCENTRATION

Any integer that can be divided evenly by a number other than itself and 1. All numbers are either prime or composite.

· ·

A substance composed of more than one element that has a definite composition and distinct physical and chemical properties. Examples include carbon dioxide, sucrose (table sugar), and serotonin (a human brain chemical).

· ·

A measure of the amount of solute that is present in a solution. A solution that contains very little solute is called *dilute*. A solution that contains a relatively large amount of solute is said to be *concentrated*.

CONCLUSION

. . . .

CONFEDERATE STATES OF AMERICA

. . . .

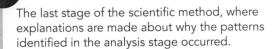

C

The last stage of the scientific method, where explanations are made about why the patterns identified in the analysis stage occurred.

. . . .

A republic formed in 1861 by 11 Southern states that withdrew from the United States. After its 1865 defeat in the American Civil War, the republic dissolved.

Free States

California	New Hampshire
Connecticut	New Jersey
Illinois	New York
Indiana	Ohio
Iowa	Oregon
Kansas	Pennsylvania
Maine	Rhode Island
Massachusetts	Vermont
Michigan	Wisconsin
Minnesota	

Slave States

Alabama*	Mississippi*
Arkansas*	Missouri
Delaware	North Carolina*
Florida*	South Carolina*
Georgia*	Tennessee*
Kentucky	Texas*
Louisiana*	Virginia*
Maryland	

Territories

Colorado	Nevada
Dakota	New Mexico
Indian	Utah
Nebraska	Washington

*Confederate States

. . . .

CONFLICT

. . . .

CONGRUENT ANGLES

. . . .

CONJUNCTION

C

A struggle or clash between two people, forces, or ideas.

· ·

Two angles that are identical in shape and size.

· ·

A joining word such as *and*, *but*, *or*, *for*, *nor*, *so*, or *yet*.

CONJUNCTIVE ADVERB

. . . .

CONNOTATION

. . . .

CONSTELLATION

An adverb that joins independent clauses. Conjunctive adverbs are punctuated differently from regular conjunctions.

also	indeed	now
anyway	instead	otherwise
besides	likewise	similarly
certainly	meanwhile	still
finally	moreover	then
furthermore	namely	therefore
however	nevertheless	thus
incidentally	next	undoubtedly

. . . .

Implied or suggested meaning. For example, the word *slim* has a different connotation than the word *thin*; *slim* suggests more grace and class than *thin*.

. . . .

An apparent grouping of stars in the sky that is used for identification purposes. These stars are not necessarily near each other in space, since they are not necessarily the same distance from Earth.

CONSTITUTION

. . . .

**CONSTITUTION OF THE
UNITED STATES**

. . . .

The fundamental principles of a nation's government embodied in one document or several documents.

. . . .

The fundamental laws of the United States, written in 1787 and ratified in 1788.

. . . .

CONSUMER PRICE INDEX (CPI)

. . . .

CONTEXT

. . . .

A measure of change in the cost of common goods and services, such as food, clothing, rent, fuel, and others.

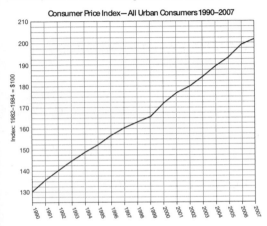

Consumer Price Index—All Urban Consumers 1990–2007

Index: 1982–1984 = $100

210
200
190
180
170
160
150
140
130

1990 1991 1992 1993 1994 1995 1996 1997 1998 1999 2000 2001 2002 2003 2004 2005 2006 2007

The graph shows the CPI in all U.S. cities between 1990 and 2007. To make comparisons between years, the graph uses the years 1982–1984 as a base period (1982–1984 = $100). For instance, if the average urban consumer spent $100 on living expenses in 1982–1984, he or she spent more than $150 on the same expenses in 1995.

• •

The words and sentences surrounding a word or phrase that help determine the meaning of that word or phrase.

• •

CONTINENTAL CONGRESS

. . . .

CONTINENTAL DRIFT

. . . .

CONVERGENT BOUNDARY

An assembly of delegates from the American colonies who served as a governmental body that directed the war for independence.

· ·

The region on a continent where new crust is being created and the plates on either side of the rift are moving apart.

· ·

A boundary between two of Earth's plates that are moving toward each other.

COORDINATE PLANE

A graph formed by two lines that intersect to create right angles.

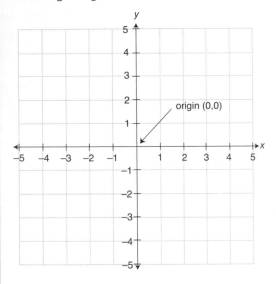

origin (0,0)

COORDINATE POINT

. . . .

COPLANAR

. . . .

A specific point on the coordinate plane with the first number, or coordinate, representing the horizontal placement and the second number, or coordinate, representing the vertical. Coordinate points are given in the form of (x,y). Also called an *ordered pair*.

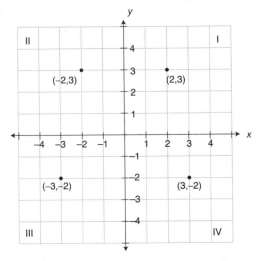

Points that lie together on a common plane or grid.

COSMOLOGY

. . . .

COST OF LIVING

. . . .

COUNCIL-MANAGER

C

The study of the formation of the universe.

. . . .

The price of common goods and services that are considered living expenses, such as food, clothing, rent, fuel, and others.

. . . .

A form of local government in which voters elect council members, who, in turn, hire a manager to run the day-to-day operations of the locality.

COUNTING NUMBERS

. . . .

COUPLET

. . . .

CRUSADES

All whole numbers, with the exception of 0.

· ·

A pair of rhyming lines in poetry.

· ·

Any of the military campaigns led by European Christians during the Middle Ages to recover the Holy Land from Muslims.

CRYSTAL

. . . .

CULTURAL GEOGRAPHY

. . . .

CULTURE

A solid in which atoms or molecules have a regular repeated arrangement.

. . . .

The study of the relationship between humans and their physical environment.

. . . .

A shared way of living among a group of people that develops over time.

CURRENT

. . . .

CUTICLE

. . . .

CYTOPLASM

C

The flow of charge past a point per unit time; current is measured in amperes (A).

. . . .

The top layer on a leaf. The cuticle is a non-living layer consisting primarily of wax that is produced by the epithelium, a cell layer directly underneath.

. . . .

A jelly-like substance located in the cell where all of the internal organelles can be found. The cytoplasm consists primarily of water and supports the cell and its organelles.

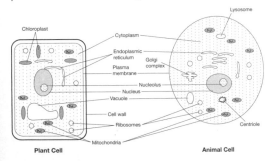

Plant Cell   Animal Cell

CYTOSKELETON

· ·

Organelles that are the internal "bones" of the cell. The cytoskeleton consists of thick and thin tubules.

. . . .

DANGLING MODIFIERS

. . . .

DECIBEL

. . . .

D

Words, phrases, or clauses that begin a sentence and are set off by commas, but mistakenly modify the wrong noun or pronoun.

Examples:

Incorrect: *Worn and tattered, Uncle Joe took down the flag.*

Correct: *Uncle Joe took down the flag, which was worn and tattered.* OR *Uncle Joe took down the worn, tattered flag.*

Incorrect: *While making breakfast, the smoke alarm went off and woke the baby.*

Correct: *While I was making breakfast, the smoke alarm went off and woke the baby.* OR *The smoke alarm went off and woke the baby while I was making breakfast.*

. . . .

A unit of measure for the relative intensity of sounds.

. . . .

DECIMAL

....

**DECLARATION OF
INDEPENDENCE**

....

A number in the base-10 number system. Each place value in a decimal number is worth ten times the place value of the digit to its right.

1	2	6	8	•	3	4	5	7
T H O U S A N D S	H U N D R E D S	T E N S	O N E S	D E C I M A L POINT	T E N T H S	H U N D R E D T H S	T H O U S A N D T H S	T E N T H O U S A N D T H S

In expanded form, this number can also be expressed as:

1,268.3457 = (1 × 1,000) + (2 × 100) + (6 × 10) + (8 × 1) + (3 × .1) + (4 × .01) + (5 × .001) + (7 × .0001)

. . . .

A document adopted on July 4, 1776, in which the American colonies proclaimed their independence from Great Britain.

. . . .

DECLINATION

. . . .

DEFLATION

. . . .

DELTA

D

The celestial coordinate similar to that of latitude on Earth. Declination measures how many degrees, minutes, and seconds north or south of the celestial equator an object is.

· ·

A decrease in prices due to decreased money supply and an increased quantity of consumer goods.

· ·

A fan-shaped deposit of material at the mouth of a river.

DEMAND

. . . .

DEMOCRACY

. . . .

DEMOGRAPHY

GED® TEST FLASH REVIEW

The quantity of goods or services that consumers want to buy at any given price. According to the principle of demand, demand decreases as price increases, and vice versa.

. . . .

A form of government in which decisions are made by the people, either directly or through elected representatives.

Characteristics	Examples
• In *representative democracy*, people elect officials to represent their views. • In *direct democracy*, decisions are made by the people.	*Representative:* • United States • Canada • Most European nations *Direct:* • Switzerland

. . . .

The study of changes in population through birth rate, death rate, migration, and other factors.

DENITRIFICATION

. . . .

DENOMINATOR

. . . .

DENOTATION

D

A process in which bacteria convert nitrites or nitrates back into nitrogen gas, which is then released into the atmosphere.

· ·

The bottom number in a fraction. The denominator of $\frac{1}{2}$ is 2.

· ·

Exact or dictionary meaning. For example, the words *slim* and *thin* have a similar denotation.

DENOUEMENT

. . . .

DENSITY

. . . .

DEPRESSION

The resolution or conclusion of the action.

. . . .

The mass of a substance for a given unit volume. A common unit of density is grams per milliliter (g/ml).

. . . .

A prolonged and severe period of low economic productivity and incomes.

DIAGONAL

. . . .

DIALECT

. . . .

DIALOGUE

D

Symbol (/) used to join words or numbers. The most frequent use of the diagonal is with the phrase *and/or*, which shows that the sentence refers to one or both of the words being joined. Diagonals are also used to separate numbers in a fraction, to show line division in poetry, or to indicate *per* or *divided by*. Also known as a *backslash*.

. . . .

Language that differs from the standard language in grammar, pronunciation, and idioms (natural speech versus standard English); language used by a specific group within a culture.

. . . .

The verbal exchange between two or more people; a conversation.

DIAMETER

. . . .

DICTATORSHIP

. . . .

A line segment that goes directly through the center of a circle and has endpoints on the curve of the circle. A diameter is the longest line you can draw in a circle.

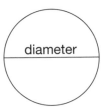

. . . .

A form of government in which one ruler has absolute power over many aspects of society, including social, economic, and political life.

Characteristics	Examples
• It is ruled by one leader who has absolute power over many aspects of life, including social, economic, and political. • Leader is not elected by the people.	• Nazi (National Socialist) government of Adolf Hitler • General Augusto Pinochet in Chile from 1973–1990 • North Korea

. . . .

DICTION

. . . .

DIFFERENCE

. . . .

DIRECT ELECTION

D

The particular choice and use of appropriate words, combining them in the right way to communicate your message accurately.

. . . .

The result of subtracting one number from another. For example, the difference between $800 and $500 is $300. $800 − $500 = $300

These words . . .	. . . often translate into these math symbols
subtracted from	−
difference	
decreased by	
minus	
take away	
less	

. . . .

A type of electoral process in which the citizens of a state or country elect the government officials and representatives.

DISCOUNT RATE

. . . .

DISPLACEMENT

. . . .

DISTANCE

D

The interest rate that the U.S. Federal Reserve Board charges banks to borrow money.

. . . .

The change in position of an object, computed by calculating the final position minus the initial position. Common units of measure are meters (m).

. . . .

Distance = rate × time

DISTANCE BETWEEN POINTS ON A COORDINATE PLANE

. . . .

(x_1, y_1) and (x_2, y_2) are two points on the line. The distance between two points is the length of the path connecting them. In the plane, the distance between points (x_1, y_1) and (x_2, y_2) is given by the distance formula:

$$d = \sqrt{(x_2 - x_1)^2 + (y_2 - y_1)^2}$$

Example:

What is the distance between the points $(-2, 8)$ and $(4, -2)$?

Substitute these values into the formula:

$$\begin{aligned}
D &= \sqrt{[4 - (-2)]^2 + [(-2) - 8]^2} \\
&= \sqrt{(4 + 2)^2 + (-2 - 8)^2} \\
&= \sqrt{(6)^2 + (-10)^2} \\
&= \sqrt{36 + 100} \\
&= \sqrt{136}
\end{aligned}$$

GED® TEST FLASH REVIEW

DISTRIBUTIVE PROPERTY

. . . .

DIVERGENT BOUNDARY

. . . .

DIVIDEND

D

This property states that multiplication distributes over addition or subtraction. In other words, $a \times (b + c) = (a \times b) + (a \times c)$.

Example:

$17 \times 5 =$

You know that $7 + 10 = 17$: 17×5
$= 5(10 + 7)$.

Use the distributive property: $5 \times 10 + 5 \times 7$.

Follow the order of operations: $50 + 35$
$= 85$.

· ·

A boundary between two of Earth's plates that are moving away from each other.

· ·

The number in a division problem that is being divided. In $32 \div 4 = 8$, 32 is the dividend.

DIVISIBLE BY

. . . .

DNA

. . . .

DOUBLE NEGATIVE

D

Capable of being evenly divided by a given number, without a remainder.

. . . .

Abbreviation for deoxyribonucleic acid. Contains all genetic material for an organism. The smallest units of DNA are called nucleotides.

. . . .

A negative word added to a statement that is already negative. For example, *I don't want nothing.*

Examples:

Incorrect: *He doesn't have no idea what she's talking about.*

Correct: *He doesn't have any idea what she's talking about.*

  OR

  He has no idea what she's talking about.

DRAMA

. . . .

DRAMATIC IRONY

. . . .

DRED SCOTT DECISION

D

Literature that is meant to be performed.

· ·

When a character's speech or actions have an unintended meaning that is known to the audience but not to the character.

· ·

An 1857 U.S. Supreme Court decision that ruled that the Court could not ban citizens from bringing slaves into free territories.

ECLIPTIC

....

ELECTORAL COLLEGE

....

The apparent path of the sun across the sky over the course of a year.

• •

The system by which the President of the United States is elected, wherein the electors of each state cast their electoral votes for the winner of the popular vote in their state. Currently, a presidential candidate needs 270 electoral votes to win the election.

Presidential Electoral Vote — November 2004
Total electoral votes: Bush 286, Kerry 252.

George W. Bush and
Richard B. Cheney

John Kerry and
John Edwards

The electoral college is a group of electors who choose the president and vice president. Each state is allowed the same number of electors as its total number of U.S. senators and representatives—so each state has at least three electors. In most states, the candidate who wins the most popular votes earns that state's electoral votes.
Source: National Archives and Records Administration.

• •

ELECTRICAL POTENTIAL ENERGY

. . . .

ELECTROMAGNETIC WAVE

. . . .

ELECTROSTATIC FORCE

E

The energy due to an object's position within an electric field.

· ·

A light wave that has an electric field component and a magnetic field component. An electromagnetic wave does not require a medium through which to travel.

· ·

The force that exists between particles due to their charges. Particles of like charge repel, particles of unlike charge attract.

ELEGY

. . . .

E

A poem that laments the loss of someone or something.

. . . .

ELEMENT

A pure chemical substance consisting of one type of atom. It cannot be decomposed by ordinary chemical reactions.

Examples:

H—Hydrogen: involved in the nuclear process that produces energy in the sun, found in many organic molecules within our bodies (like fats and carbohydrates) and in gases (like methane)

He—Helium: used to make balloons fly

C—Carbon: found in all living organisms; pure carbon exists as graphite and diamonds

N—Nitrogen: used as a coolant to rapidly freeze food, found in many biologically important molecules, such as proteins

O—Oxygen: essential for respiration (breathing) and combustion (burning)

Si—Silicon: used in making transistors and solar cells

Cl—Chlorine: used as a disinfectant in pools and as a cleaning agent in bleach, and is also important physiologically as well, as in the nervous system

Ca—Calcium: necessary for bone formation and muscle contraction

Fe—Iron: used as a building material; carries oxygen in the blood

Cu—Copper: a U.S. penny is made of copper; good conductor of electricity

I—Iodine: lack in the diet results in an enlarged thyroid gland, or goiter

Hg—Mercury: used in thermometers; ingestion can cause brain damage and poisoning

Pb—Lead: used for X-ray shielding in a dentist office

Na—Sodium: Found in table salt (NaCl), also important biologically within the nervous system and is a key player in the active transport process that occurs across cell membranes

ELLIPSE

. . . .

ELLIPSIS

. . . .

EM-DASH

E

A geometric shape that is formed when a plane intersects with a cone at an angle, so that a shape similar to a circle but stretched in one direction is formed. The orbits of the planets around the sun represent ellipses.

· ·

Symbol (...) used to show that quoted material has been omitted, or to indicate a pause or hesitation.

· ·

A specialized punctuation mark (—) that can be used to mark a sudden break in thought or to insert a comment, emphasize explanatory material, indicate omitted letters or words, or connect a beginning phrase to the rest of the sentence.

ENDOPLASMIC RETICULUM

. . . .

ENERGY

. . . .

An organelle that is used to transport proteins throughout the cell.

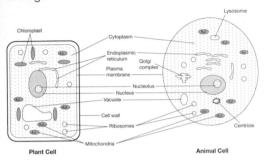

Plant Cell   Animal Cell

• •

The ability to do work or undergo change. Kinetic energy is the energy of motion, while potential energy is stored energy.

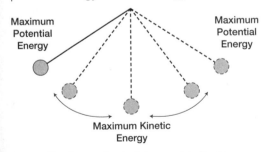

The change of potential energy into kinetic energy, and kinetic energy into potential energy, in a pendulum.

• •

ENLIGHTENMENT

. . . .

EPICYCLE

. . . .

EQUATION

E

A philosophical movement of the eighteenth century in Europe and North America that emphasized rational thought.

. . . .

Smaller circles on which the planets traveled around Earth in the geocentric model of the solar system. Epicycles were used to explain the retrograde motion of planets and help make the predicted positions of the planets match the observed positions.

. . . .

Two equal expressions.
Examples:
$2 + 2 = 1 + 3$
$2x = 4$

EQUATOR

. . . .

The imaginary line drawn around the earth that runs east and west at 0° latitude.

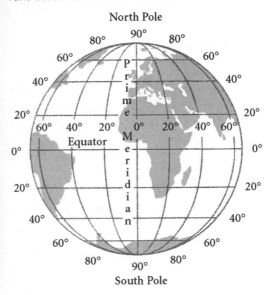

EQUIDISTANT

. . . .

EQUILATERAL TRIANGLE

. . . .

EQUILIBRIUM (CHEMISTRY)

A point between two objects where the distance between the point and each object is the same.

. . . .

A type of triangle where all sides are equal and all angles are equal.

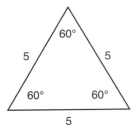

. . . .

A state at which the forward and reverse reactions proceed at the same rate.

EQUILIBRIUM (ECONOMICS)

. . . .

EVEN NUMBER

. . . .

EXACT RHYME

E

When supply of a good or service equals that which customers are willing to buy (demand).

. . . .

A counting number that is divisible by 2. Here are some helpful rules for how even and odd numbers behave when added or multiplied:

even + even = even	and	even × even = even
odd + odd = even	and	odd × odd = odd
odd + even = odd	and	even × odd = even

. . . .

The repetition of identically stressed sounds at the ends of words. (e.g., *cat* and *hat*; *laugh* and *staff*; *refine* and *divine*)

EXECUTIVE BRANCH

. . . .

EXPANDED NOTATION

. . . .

The arm of government that carries out laws.

Members	Characteristics
• President • Vice President • Agencies • Departments	• A president is elected by the voters for four-year term. • A president cannot serve more than two terms. • Vice president becomes head of state if the president becomes disabled or dies in office. • Agencies carry out a president's policies and provide special services. • Department heads advise a president and carry out policies.

• •

A method of writing numbers as the sum of their units (hundreds, tens, ones, etc.). The expanded notation for 378 is 300 + 70 + 8.

• •

EXPONENT

. . . .

EXPOSITION

. . . .

EYE RHYME

E

A number that indicates an operation of repeated multiplication. For instance, 3^2 indicates that the number 3 should be multiplied by itself once; 3^5 indicates it should be multiplied by itself four times.

$$2^5 \leftarrow \text{exponent} = 2 \times 2 \times 2 \times 2 \times 2 = 32$$
$\uparrow$
base

Exponent	Exponential Form	Standard Form
1	3^1	3
2	3^2	9
3	3^3	27
4	3^4	81
5	3^5	243

· ·

In a plot, the conveyance of background information necessary to understand the complication of the plot.

· ·

Words that look like they should rhyme because of spelling, but because of pronunciation, they do not. (e.g., *slaughter* and *laughter*; *enough* and *though*; *bough* and *through*)

FACTOR

. . . .

FALLING ACTION

. . . .

FASCISM

GED® TEST FLASH REVIEW

F

The events that take place immediately after the climax, in which "loose ends" of the plot are tied up.

· ·

One of two or more numbers or variables that are being multiplied together.

· ·

An Italian term for a military-based totalitarian government.

FEDERAL RESERVE SYSTEM (THE FED)

. . . .

FEDERALISM

. . . .

FEDERALIST PAPERS

F

U.S. banking system established in 1913. Includes 12 Federal Reserve banks under an eight-member controlling board.

· ·

A government structure that divides power between a central government and regional governments. The United States is a federal republic, a democracy that divides power between federal, state, and local governments.

· ·

A series of 85 essays written in 1787–1788 by Alexander Hamilton, James Madison, and John Jay in which they argued that federalism would offer a government structure that would preserve the rights of states and secure individual freedoms.

FEET

. . . .

FEUDALISM

. . . .

FICTION

In poetry, a group of stressed and unstressed syllables.

· ·

A political and economic system that existed in Europe between the ninth and fifteenth centuries in which a lord granted land and employment to a tenant in exchange for political and military services.

· ·

Prose literature about people, places, and events invented by the author.

FIGURATIVE LANGUAGE

. . . .

FLASHBACK

. . . .

FOCAL LENGTH

Comparisons not meant to be taken literally but used for artistic effect, including similes, metaphors, and personification.

. . . .

When an earlier event or scene is inserted into the chronology of the plot.

. . . .

The distance from a focal point to a mirror or lens.

FORCE

. . . .

FRACTAL

. . . .

F

That which acts on an object to change its motion; a push or pull exerted on one object by another. The unit of force is the Newton (N).

• •

A geometric figure that is self-similar; that is, any smaller piece of the figure will have roughly the same shape as the whole.

• •

FRACTION

F

The result of dividing two numbers. When you divide 3 by 5, you get $\frac{3}{5}$, which equals 0.6. A fraction is a way of expressing a number that involves dividing a top number (the numerator) by a bottom number (the denominator).

Decimal and Fraction Equivalents to Know	
FRACTION	DECIMAL
$\frac{1}{100}$	0.01
$\frac{1}{10}$	0.1
$\frac{1}{5}$	0.2
$\frac{1}{4}$	0.25
$\frac{1}{3}$	0.33 (rounded)
$\frac{1}{2}$	0.5
$\frac{2}{3}$	0.67 (rounded)
$\frac{3}{4}$	0.75
$\frac{4}{5}$	0.8
$\frac{9}{10}$	0.9

FREE ENTERPRISE

. . . .

FREE VERSE

. . . .

FREEFALL

F

Freedom of private business to organize and operate for profit with no or little government intervention.

. . . .

Poetry that is free from any restrictions of meter and rhyme.

. . . .

An object in one-dimensional motion that is only acted on by the force of Earth's gravity. In this case, its acceleration will be $-g$ or g downward.

FRENCH AND INDIAN WAR

. . . .

FREQUENCY

. . . .

FRICTIONAL FORCE

The last of four North American wars fought between Great Britain and France in which each country fought for control of the continent (1754–1763).

· ·

The number of cycles or repetitions per second. Frequency is often measured as the number of revolutions per second. The common units of frequency are hertz (Hz), where one hertz equals 1 cycle/second.

· ·

The force that acts parallel to surfaces in contact opposite the direction of motion or tendency of motion.

FUNCTIONAL GROUP

. . . .

FUNCTIONAL TEXTS

. . . .

FUTURE PERFECT TENSE

A group of atoms that give a molecule a certain characteristic or property.

· ·

Literature that is valued mainly for the information it conveys, not for its beauty of form, emotional impact, or message about human experience.

· ·

Verb form that shows continuing actions that will be completed at a certain time in the future. For example, "By 2020, I *will have lived* in New York for 20 years." and "By 2020, I *will have been living* in New York for 20 years."

FUTURE PROGRESSIVE TENSE

. . . .

FUTURE TENSE

. . . .

F

Verb form that shows continuing actions in the future. For example, "I *will be running* in next year's Boston Marathon."

. . . .

Verb form that shows action that has yet to happen.

. . . .

GEL ELECTROPHORESIS

. . . .

GENERAL ELECTION

. . . .

GENRE

G

A process used in laboratories to determine the genetic makeup of DNA strands. This process involves the movement of chromosomes through a gel from one pole to the other. Magnetism is used to pull the chromosomes through the gel.

· ·

An election in which the citizens of a nation or region vote to elect the ultimate winner of a political contest.

· ·

Category or kind; in literature, the different kinds or categories of texts.

GEOCENTRIC MODEL

. . . .

GEOCHEMICAL CYCLE

. . . .

G

The model of the solar system that places Earth at the center with the planets and the sun orbiting around it.

· ·

The circulation of elements in the biosphere. For example, water, carbon, and nitrogen are recycled in the biosphere. A water molecule in the cell of your eye could have been at some point in the ocean, in the atmosphere, in a leaf of a tree, or in the cell of a bear's foot.

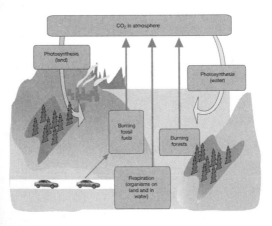

· ·

GEOLOGY

. . . .

GLACIER

. . . .

GOLGI APPARATUS

The study of rocks and minerals.

• •

A large mass of snow-covered ice.

• •

An organelle that packages proteins so that they can be sent out of the cell. Also called *Golgi complex*.

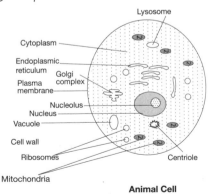

Lysosome

Cytoplasm

Endoplasmic reticulum

Golgi complex

Plasma membrane

Nucleolus

Nucleus

Vacuole

Cell wall

Ribosomes

Centriole

Mitochondria

Animal Cell

GOVERNMENT

. . . .

GRAVITATIONAL FORCE

. . . .

GREAT DEPRESSION

G

The act or process of governing; the control of public policy within a political organization.

. . . .

The attractive force that exists between all particles with mass.

. . . .

A severe economic recession characterized by bank closings, failed businesses, high unemployment, and homelessness that lasted through the 1930s in the United States.

GREENHOUSE EFFECT

. . . .

**GROSS DOMESTIC PRODUCT
(GDP)**

. . . .

**GROSS NATIONAL PRODUCT
(GNP)**

G

A process whereby carbon dioxide in the atmosphere can trap solar energy. The trapped heat causes a rise in global temperature.

. . . .

A measure of the total value of goods and services produced within a nation over the course of a year.

. . . .

A measure of the value of goods and services produced within a nation as well as its foreign investments over the course of a year.

HAIKU

· ·

HALF-RHYME

· ·

HELIOCENTRIC MODEL

H

A short, imagistic poem of three unrhymed lines of five, seven, and five syllables, respectively.

· ·

The repetition of the final consonant at the end of words (e.g., *cat* and *hot*; *adamant* and *government*; *soul* and *all*).

· ·

The model of the solar system that places the sun at the center with the planets orbiting around it.

HEMISPHERE

. . . .

HETEROGENEOUS MIXTURE

. . . .

HEXAGON

H

Half of Earth; either the northern or southern half of the globe as divided by the equator or the eastern and western half as divided by the prime meridian.

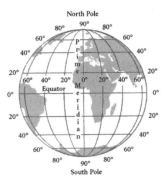

· ·

A mixture that is not uniform in composition. An example is a mixture of salt and pepper.

· ·

A polygon with six sides.

GED® TEST FLASH REVIEW

[200]

HIROSHIMA

. . . .

HOLOCAUST

. . . .

HOMOGENEOUS MIXTURE

A city in southwestern Japan that was the target of the first atomic bomb ever dropped on a populated area in August 1945.

· ·

Persecution and murder of millions of Jewish people and other Europeans under Adolf Hitler's Nazi regime.

· ·

A mixture in which the components are uniformly distributed. An example is a mixture of a small amount of salt in water.

HOMONYM

. . . .

HUMANISM

. . . .

HYDRATEA

H

A set of distinct words with different meanings and spellings that are pronounced alike. For example, *sea* and *see*.

. . . .

A cultural and intellectual movement of the Renaissance that emphasized classical ideals as a result of a rediscovery of ancient Greek and Roman literature and art.

. . . .

Crystal of a molecule that also contains water in the crystal structure. If the water evaporates, the crystal becomes anhydrous.

HYDROLOGY

. . . .

HYPERBOLE

. . . .

HYPHEN

H

The study of Earth's water and water systems.

· ·

Extreme exaggeration not meant to be taken literally, but done for effect. For example, "I am so hungry I could eat a horse."

· ·

Symbol (-) used to join words in creating compound nouns or adjectives. Hyphens can be used to: join two coequal nouns working together as one (e.g., teacher-poet); join multi-word compound nouns (e.g., up-to-date); join two or more words that function as a single adjective preceding the noun (e.g., a soft-spoken person); and join prefixes and suffixes to words (e.g., ex-husband, secretary-elect).

HYPOTENUSE

. . . .

HYPOTHESIS

. . . .

The longest leg of a right triangle that is always opposite the right angle.

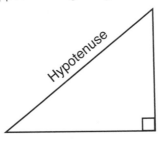

. . . .

The step in the scientific method where a prediction is made about the end result of an experiment. A hypothesis is generally based on research of related data.

. . . .

IAMBIC PENTAMETER

. . . .

IGNEOUS ROCK

. . . .

IMAGE DISTANCE

A metrical pattern in poetry in which each line has 10 syllables (five feet) and the stress falls on every second syllable. The *da-dum* of a human heartbeat is the most common example of this rhythm: *da-dum*, *da-dum*, *da-dum*.

• •

A rock formed through the cooling of magma.

• •

The distance from an image to a mirror or lens.

IMAGERY

. . . .

IMMIGRATION

. . . .

IMPERIALISM

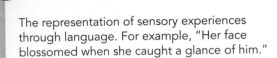

The representation of sensory experiences through language. For example, "Her face blossomed when she caught a glance of him."

. . . .

The process of moving and settling in a country or region to which one is not native.

. . . .

The practice of extending a nation's power by territorial acquisition or by economic and political influence over other nations.

IMPROPER FRACTION

. . . .

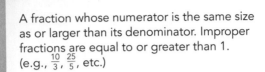

A fraction whose numerator is the same size as or larger than its denominator. Improper fractions are equal to or greater than 1. (e.g., $\frac{10}{3}$, $\frac{25}{5}$, etc.)

Example:

Convert $\frac{62}{8}$ to a mixed number.

Find how many times 8 divides into 62:

$$
\begin{array}{r}
7 \\
8\overline{)62} \\
56 \\
\hline
6R
\end{array}
$$

Find the whole number part: 7.

Find the remainder: 6.

The mixed number is $7\frac{6}{8}$ or $7\frac{3}{4}$.

· ·

INDEPENDENT CLAUSE

. . . .

INDUSTRIAL REVOLUTION

. . . .

A group of words within a sentence that by itself could form a complete sentence.

Independent clause: *She was excited.*

Dependent clause: *Because she was excited.*

Notice that the dependent clause is incomplete; it needs an additional thought to make a complete sentence, such as:

She spoke very quickly *because she was excited.*

The independent clause, however, can stand alone. It is a complete thought.

. . . .

The extensive social and economic changes brought about by the shift from the manufacturing of goods by hand to large-scale factory production that began in England in the late eighteenth century.

. . . .

INEQUALITY

. . . .

Two expressions that are not equal and are described by an inequality symbol such as <, >, ≤, ≥, or ≠.

A conclusion based upon reason, fact, or evidence.

Example:

If $7 - 2x > 21$, find x.

Isolate the variable:

$7 - 2x > 21$

$7 - 2x - 7 > 21 - 7$

$-2x > 14$

Then divide both sides by –2. Because you are dividing by a negative number, the inequality symbol changes direction: $\frac{-2x}{-2} > \frac{14}{-2}$ becomes $x < -7$, so the answer consists of all real numbers less than –7.

. . . .

INERTIA

....

INFERENCE

....

INFINITIVE PHRASE

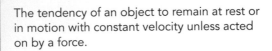

The tendency of an object to remain at rest or in motion with constant velocity unless acted on by a force.

· ·

A conclusion based upon reason, fact, or evidence.

· ·

A phrase that begins with the infinitive form of a verb (one which follows the word *to*) that functions as a noun, an adjective, or an adverb in a sentence. For example, "He helped *to build the roof.*"

INFLATION

. . . .

INORGANIC

. . . .

INTEGER

GED® TEST FLASH REVIEW

An increase in prices due to an increase in the amount of money in circulation and a decreased supply of consumer goods.

· ·

A material that is neither plant nor animal in origin.

· ·

All of the whole numbers, including negatives. Examples are –3, –2, –1, 0, 1, 2, and 3. Note that integers do not include fractions or decimals. Here are some rules for working with integers:

$(+) \times (+) = +$	$(+) \div (+) = +$	$(+) + (+) = +$
$(+) \times (-) = -$	$(+) \div (-) = -$	$(-) + (-) = -$
$(-) \times (-) = +$	$(-) \div (-) = +$	$(+) - (-) = +$
		$(-) - (+) = -$

Example:

$8 + -11 =$

Subtract the absolute values of the numbers:

$11 - 8 = 3$

The sign of the larger number (11) was originally negative, so the answer is –3.

INTENSITY

. . . .

INTEREST

. . . .

INTOLERABLE ACTS

The power per unit area of a wave; measured in Watts/m^2.

. . . .

The price paid for the use of borrowed money.

. . . .

A series of laws passed by the British Parliament in 1774 to punish the colony of Massachusetts for the Boston Tea Party.

ION

....

IRONY

....

ISOLATIONISM

An atom that has either lost electrons to become a positively charged *cation*, or has gained electrons to become a negatively charged *anion*. For example, calcium (Ca) can lose two electrons to become an ion with a positive charge of +2 (Ca^{2+})

· ·

The use of words to express something other than and especially the opposite of the literal meaning.

· ·

A national policy of avoiding political alliances with other nations.

ISOMERS

. . . .

ISOSCELES TRIANGLE

. . . .

ISOTOPES

Substances that have the same molecular formula (same number of elements) in different arrangements.

· ·

A type of triangle that has two sides the same length, where equal angles are opposite equal sides.

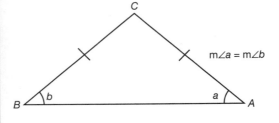

$m\angle a = m\angle b$

· ·

Atoms of the same element, with different numbers of neutrons, and hence different atomic masses.

JARGON

. . . .

JOVIAN PLANETS

. . . .

J

Technical, wordy language used by those associated with a trade or profession.

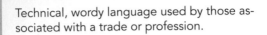

The outer planets of the solar system that have characteristics similar to those of Jupiter. The Jovian planets are Jupiter, Saturn, Uranus, and Neptune. They are large, have many moons, and may have rings. They have thick atmospheres, are gaseous, and have high mass and low density. Jovian planets are located far from the sun and from each other. They have a composition similar to that of the sun, have short rotation rates, and have long revolution periods around the sun. Jovian planets are also called *gas planets*.

JUDICIAL BRANCH

. . . .

JUDICIAL REVIEW

. . . .

J

The arm of government that interprets laws.

Members	Characteristics
• U.S. Supreme Court • Circuit Courts of Appeals • Federal District Courts	• U.S. Supreme Court is the highest court in the nation. • The president appoints the nine justices of the Supreme Court. • Term is for life.

. . . .

A doctrine that allows the U.S. Supreme Court to invalidate laws and executive actions if the Court decides they conflict with the Constitution. This power was not established until the 1803 case of *Marbury v. Madison*.

. . . .

KINETIC ENERGY

. . . .

The energy due to an object's motion or velocity.

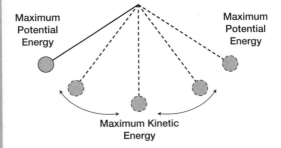

The change of potential energy into kinetic energy, and kinetic energy into potential energy, in a pendulum.

. . . .

LABOR MARKET

. . . .

LABOR UNION

. . . .

LAISSEZ-FAIRE

L

The market in which workers compete for jobs and employers compete for workers. As in other markets, the labor market is driven by supply and demand.

. . . .

An organization of wage earners that uses group action to seek better economic and working conditions.

. . . .

A doctrine that believes economic systems work better without intervention by government.

LAND BREEZE

. . . .

LATITUDE

. . . .

The breeze that develops on the shoreline due to unequal heating of the air above the land and ocean. Land breeze occurs at night when the air above the land is cooler and the air above the ocean is warmer. The breeze blows from the land to the sea.

. . . .

The coordinate used to measure positions on Earth north or south of the equator, ranging from 0° at the equator to 90° at the poles. Latitude is measured in degrees, minutes, and seconds.

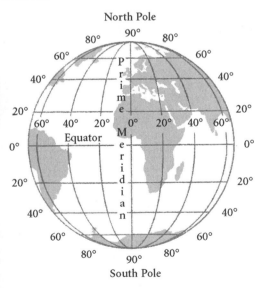

LEGEND

. . . .

LEGISLATIVE BRANCH

. . . .

LIKE TERMS

A table or list that explains the symbols used on a map or chart.

. . . .

The law-making arm of a government.

Members	Characteristics
• U.S. Congress: • House of Representatives • Senate	• Number of representatives for each state is based on the population of that state. • Representatives serve two-year terms. • Each state has two senators. • Senators serve six-year terms.

. . . .

Terms that have the same variable(s) with the same exponent(s), such as $3x^2y$ and $5x^2y$.

Like Terms	What Both Terms Contain
$5x$ and $9x$	x
$3x^2$ and $8x^2$	x^2
xy and $-5xy$	xy

LINE

. . . .

LINEAR EQUATION

. . . .

L

An infinite collection of points in a straight path.

. . . .

An equation for a straight line. The variable in a linear equation cannot contain an exponent greater than 1. This type of equation cannot have a variable in the denominator, and the variables cannot be multiplied.

Example:

Solve the following linear equation:

$x + 5 = 10$.

What operation is used in the equation? Addition. In order to get the x alone, you will need to get rid of the 5. So, you should use the inverse operation and subtract. Remember, you have to perform the operation to both sides of the equation:

$x + 5 = 10$
$ -5 -5$ → Subtract 5 from both sides
of the equation.

Combine like terms on both sides of the equal sign:

$x + 5 = 10$
$ -5 -5$
$x + 0 = 5$ → All like terms have been
combined.

Therefore, $x = 5$.

. . . .

LITERARY TEXTS

. . . .

LITERATURE

. . . .

L

Literature valued for its beauty of form, emotional impact, and message(s) about the human experience.

. . . .

Any written or published text.

. . . .

LONGITUDE

....

The coordinate used to measure positions on Earth east or west of the prime meridian, ranging from 0° at the prime meridian to 180° east or 180° west longitude. The prime meridian goes through Greenwich, England. Longitude is measured in degrees, minutes, and seconds.

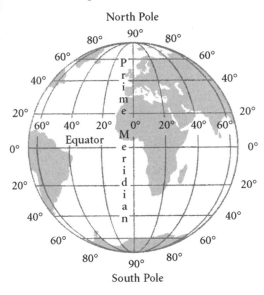

LONGITUDINAL WAVE

. . . .

LOUISIANA PURCHASE

. . . .

L

A wave that has the same direction of vibration as its direction of travel. The motion of the particles in the medium is parallel to the direction of wave propagation. Sound is an example of a longitudinal wave.

· ·

The vast land area in North America bought by the United States from France in 1803.

· ·

MAIN IDEA

. . . .

MARKET

. . . .

MASS

The overall fact, feeling, or thought a writer wants to convey about his or her subject.

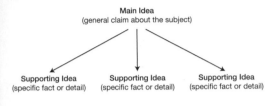

Main Idea
(general claim about the subject)

Supporting Idea
(specific fact or detail)

Supporting Idea
(specific fact or detail)

Supporting Idea
(specific fact or detail)

• •

Any forum in which an exchange between buyers and sellers takes place.

• •

The amount of matter in an object; also a measure of the amount of inertia of an object. The unit of mass is the kilogram (kg).

MAYFLOWER COMPACT

. . . .

MAYOR-COUNCIL

. . . .

MEAN

An agreement which stated that the settlers of the Plymouth Colony would make decisions by the will of the majority. It is the first instance of self-government in America.

. . . .

A form of local government in which voters elect a mayor as city or town executive and elect a council member from each ward.

. . . .

$(x_1 + x_2 + \ldots + x_n - x_1) \div n$, where xs are values for which a mean is desired and n is the total number of values for x.

$$\text{mean} = \frac{\text{sum of the numbers}}{\text{the number of numbers}}$$

Example:

Find the mean of the following set of numbers: 5, 7, 19, 12, 4, 11, 15.

Add all the numbers in the list:
$5 + 7 + 19 + 12 + 4 + 11 + 15 = 73$.

Count how many numbers are in the list: There are seven numbers in the list: 7

Divide the sum by the number of numbers:
$73 \div 7 = 10.4$.

So, the mean is 10.4.

MEANDER

. . . .

MEASURES OF CENTRAL TENDENCY

. . . .

MEDIAN

A broad curve in a river.

. . . .

A single value that attempts to describe a set of data by specifying the central position within that set of data.

. . . .

The middle value of an odd number of ordered scores, and halfway between the two middle values of an even number of ordered scores.

Example:

Find the median of the following set of numbers: 5, 7, 19, 12, 4, 11, 15.

Put the numbers in sequential order: 4, 5, 7, 11, 12, 15, 19.

The middle number is the median: 11.

The median is 11.

MEIOSIS

. . . .

MELODRAMA

. . . .

MEMOIR

A process of cellular reproduction where the daughter cells have half the amount of chromosomes. This is used for purposes of sexual reproduction to produce sex cells that will be able to form an offspring with a complete set of chromosomes with different DNA than the parents.

. . . .

A play propelled by exaggerated emotion and action, with a happy ending.

. . . .

An autobiographical text that focuses on a limited number of events and explores their impact on the author.

MENISCUS

. . . .

METAMORPHIC ROCK

. . . .

METAPHOR

M

The curved surface of a liquid in a container, caused by surface tension.

. . . .

A rock whose crystal structure has been changed through heat and/or pressure.

. . . .

A type of figurative language that compares two things by saying they are equal. Take, for example, the expression, "He is the apple of my eye." There is, of course, no real apple in a person's eye. The "apple" is someone beloved and held dear.

METEOROLOGY

. . . .

METER

. . . .

MIDDLE AGES

The study of Earth's atmosphere and weather.

. . . .

The number and stress of syllables in a line of poetry.

. . . .

A period in Europe beginning with the decline of the Roman Empire in the fifth century and ending with the Renaissance in 1453.

MID-OCEANIC RIDGE

. . . .

A region under the ocean where new crust is being created and the plates on either side of the ridge are moving apart.

. . . .

MIDPOINT

· ·

The middle point of a line segment.

Example:

Find the midpoint of line segment *AB*.

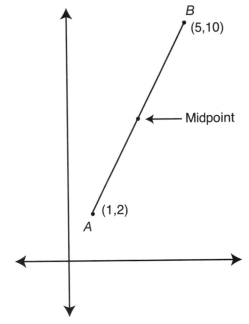

Midpoint x = $\frac{(1 + 5)}{2}$ = $\frac{6}{2}$ = 3

Midpoint y = $\frac{(2 + 10)}{2}$ = $\frac{12}{2}$ = 6

Therefore, the midpoint of $\overline{AB}$ is (3,6).

MINERAL

. . . .

M

A naturally occurring element or compound found in Earth's crust.

Mineral	Function	Food Sources
Calcium	builds healthy bones and teeth; helps nerves and muscles	milk; cheese; green, leafy vegetables; fish; eggs
Iodine	helps body use energy	iodized salt; fish; seafood
Iron	keeps red blood cells healthy	liver; meat; green, leafy vegetables; eggs
Magnesium	helps muscles and nerves	vegetables; cereals; meat; nuts; milk
Sodium	controls water balance; helps nerves	salt, most processed foods

MISPLACED MODIFIERS

. . . .

MITOCHONDRIA

. . . .

MITOSIS

Words, phrases, or clauses that describe nouns and pronouns, but are placed too far away (in a sentence) from the words they describe. For example, the words *only*, *almost*, and *just* should be placed as closely as possible to the words they describe.

. . . .

An organelle that produces ATP.

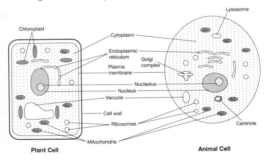

Plant Cell   Animal Cell

. . . .

A process in which cells produce genetically identical offspring.

MIXED NUMBER

. . . .

MIXTURE

. . . .

MODE

A number with an integer part and a fractional part. Mixed numbers can be converted into improper fractions. For example, the mixed number $5\frac{1}{2}$ can be converted into the improper fraction $\frac{11}{2}$.

. . . .

A physical combination of different substances.

. . . .

The value that appears most often in a data set.

Example:

Find the mode of the following set of numbers: 5, 7, 19, 12, 4, 11, 15.

None of the numbers occurs more than once, so there is no mode.

MODIFIERS

. . . .

MOLE

. . . .

MOLECULAR MASS

Words and phrases that describe other words. For example, an *adjective* is a modifier because it describes nouns and pronouns. *Adverbs* are modifiers because they describe verbs, adjectives, and other adverbs.

. . . .

The amount of a substance that contains as many particles (e.g., atoms, molecules, ions, electrons) as there are atoms in 12 grams of the carbon-12 isotope. This corresponds to a value of 6.022×10^{23} particles of the substance.

. . . .

The sum of the atomic masses in a molecule.

MOLECULE

. . . .

MONARCHY

. . . .

MONOLOGUE

M

A substance formed by a chemical bond between two or more atoms.

. . . .

A form of government headed by one ruler who claims power through hereditary or divine right.

Characteristics	Examples
• One person from a royal family is ruler. • Power is inherited from generation to generation. • Absolute monarchs have complete authority. • *Constitutional monarchs* have limited authority; a representative democracy governs.	*Absolute monarchy:* • Swaziland • Saudi Arabia *Constitutional monarchy:* • Great Britain • Japan • Sweden • Morocco

. . . .

In drama, a play or part of a play performed by one character speaking directly to the audience.

MONOMIAL

. . . .

MONOPOLY

. . . .

M

An expression with one term (e.g., $3x^2$).

. . . .

A situation in which a specific person or enterprise owns all or nearly all of the market for a particular commodity. A monopoly is characterized by a lack of viable economic competition to produce a good or service. Because losing customers to competitors is not an issue, the specific person or enterprise can set a price that is significantly higher than the cost of producing the good or service.

. . . .

MONOTHEISTIC

The worship or belief in a single God. Mono-theistic religious systems include Christianity, Judaism, Islam, and Sikhism.

Religion	Origin	Characteristics
Judaism	Middle East, now Israel—the Jewish calendar begins with the biblical time of the Creation	• The belief in a single, all-powerful God is central to Judaism. • The Torah—the instructions believed to be handed down from God to Moses—encompasses Jewish law and custom.
Christianity	Jerusalem, now in Israel—Christian calendar begins with the birth of Jesus	• Early followers believed that Jesus fulfilled the Jewish prophesy of the Messiah. • The Gospels in the Bible's New Testament describe the teachings and life of Jesus. • Beliefs include that Jesus is the son of God and that after crucifixion, he rose from the dead.
Islam	Arabia in 622 A.D.	• Its followers, called Muslims, believe in one all-powerful God. • Muslims adhere to the codes of living set forth in the holy book of Islam, the Qur'an (Koran). • The founder of Islam was Muhammed, a prophet who lived in Mecca in the sixth century, A.D.

MULTIPLE OF

. . . .

MUTUALISM

. . . .

A multiple of a number has that number as one of its factors; 35 is a multiple of 7; it is also a multiple of 5.

. . . .

A class of relationship between two organisms in which both organisms benefit. The pollination process involving flowering plants and insects (such as bees and wasps) is the best example of this. While the insects get their food in the form of nectar from the plants, the plants benefit from pollination carried out by these insects, which helps them reproduce.

. . . .

NAGASAKI

. . . .

NARRATOR

. . . .

NATURALIZATION

A seaport in western Japan that was the target of the second atomic bomb ever dropped on a populated area in August 1945. The bombing marked the end of World War II.

. . . .

In fiction, the character or person who tells the story.

. . . .

The process by which one becomes a citizen of a new country.

NEGATIVE NUMBER

. . . .

NET FORCE

. . . .

A real number whose value is less than zero.

. . . .

The vector sum of all the forces acting on an object.

. . . .

NEW DEAL

. . . .

NEWTON

. . . .

N

A domestic reform program initiated by the administration of President Franklin D. Roosevelt to provide relief and recovery from the Great Depression.

The New Deal
Agricultural Adjustment Act—paid farmers to slow their production in order to stabilize food prices
National Industrial Recovery Act—outlined codes for fair competition in industry
Securities and Exchange Commission—established to regulate stock market
Federal Deposit Insurance Corporation—insured bank deposits in the case that banks fail
Public Works Administration—built roads, public buildings, dams
Tennessee Valley Authority—brought electric power to parts of the Southeast

The metric and System International unit of force. One Newton equals one kg/s^2.

NITRIFICATION

. . . .

NOMINATIVE CASE

. . . .

NONFICTION

A process where bacteria break down ammonium ion into another set of molecules (nitrite and nitrate), resulting in a low amount of fixed nitrogen in soil.

. . . .

The case of a noun or pronoun used as the subject or a complement following a linking verb (*am, is, are, was, were*—any form of *be*).

. . . .

Prose literature about real people, places, and events.

NON-RENEWABLE RESOURCE

. . . .

NONRESTRICTIVE CLAUSE

. . . .

NORMAL FORCE

A resource that is not replaced in nature as quickly as it is used. In many cases, it is not replaced or re-formed at all. Fossil fuels such as oil and coal are examples.

. . . .

Group of words that simply adds information, but is not essential to the basic meaning of a sentence (if it is removed, the basic meaning of the sentence is not changed). Nonrestrictive clauses must be set off by commas. Also known as a *nonessential clause*.

. . . .

This force acts between any two surfaces in contact. It is the part of the contact force that acts normal or perpendicular to the surfaces in contact.

NUCLEOLUS

. . . .

NUCLEOTIDE

. . . .

An organelle found inside a nucleus that is responsible for the production of ribosomes.

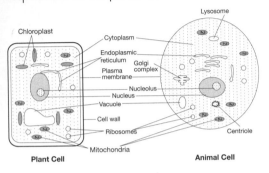

Plant Cell　　　　**Animal Cell**

. . . .

The smallest unit of DNA. There are five different types of nucleotides: adenine (A), guanine (G), thymine (T), cytosine (C), and uracil (U). The arrangement of genes is based directly on the specific arrangement of nucleotides.

. . . .

NUCLEUS

. . . .

NUMERATOR

. . . .

An organelle in a cell that contains all DNA and controls the functions of the cell.

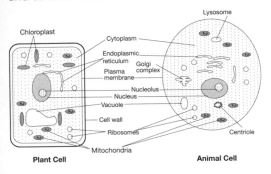

Plant Cell **Animal Cell**

· ·

The top number in a fraction. The numerator of $\frac{1}{4}$ is 1.

· ·

OBJECT DISTANCE

. . . .

OBJECTIVE CASE PRONOUN

. . . .

OBTUSE ANGLE

The distance from an object to a mirror or lens.

. . . .

Word used as the object following an action verb or as the object of a preposition.

. . . .

An angle that measures more than 90° but less than 180°.

Obtuse Angle

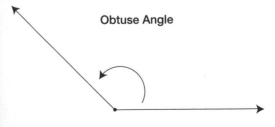

OCEANOGRAPHY

. . . .

OCTAGON

. . . .

ODD NUMBER

The study of Earth's oceans.

· ·

A polygon with eight sides.

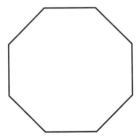

· ·

A counting number that is not divisible by 2.
Here are some helpful rules for how odd
and even numbers behave when added or
multiplied:

even + even = even	and	even × even = even
odd + odd = even	and	odd × odd = odd
odd + even = odd	and	even × odd = even

ODE

. . . .

OLIGARCHY

. . . .

OMNISCIENT NARRATOR

A poem that celebrates a person, place, or thing.

• •

A form of government in which decisions are made by a small, elite group that is not elected by the people.

Characteristics	Examples
• It is governed by a small upper-class group. • Leaders are not elected by the general populace.	• City-state of Sparta in ancient Greece • Apartheid-era South Africa

• •

A third-person narrator who knows and reveals the thoughts and feelings of the characters.

ONOMATOPOEIA

. . . .

ORBIT

. . . .

ORDER OF OPERATIONS

When the sound of a word echoes its meaning.
(e.g., *bang*, *beep*, *splash*).

· ·

The path an object takes as it travels around
another object in space.

· ·

The sequence of performing steps to get the correct answer
in a given mathematical expression. The order you follow is:
  1. Simplify all operations within grouping symbols such
     as parentheses, brackets, braces, and fraction bars.
  2. Evaluate all exponents.
  3. Do all multiplication and division in order from left to
     right.
  4. Do all addition and subtraction in order from left to
     right.

Example:

$(36 + 64) \div (18 - 20)$

First, evaluate the parentheses, from left to right:
$(36 + 64) = 100$ and $(18 - 20) = -2$.

Now, do the division: $100 \div -2 = -50$.

ORDERED PAIR

. . . .

ORGANIC

. . . .

Two numbers in a specific sequence that represent a point on a coordinate plane. The numbers are enclosed in parentheses with the x-coordinate first and the y-coordinate second; for example, (2,3). If the x-coordinate is positive, move to the right. If negative, move to the left. If the y-coordinate is positive, move up. If negative, move down.

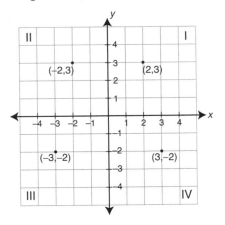

Matter or material that is plant or animal in origin.

ORIGIN

. . . .

OXBOW LAKE

. . . .

The starting point, or zero, on a number line. On a coordinate plane, the origin is the point where the x-axis and y-axis intersect. The coordinates of the origin are (0,0).

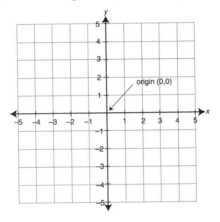

A crescent-shaped lake formed when a meander is cut off from the river it was part of.

OXIDATION

. . . .

The loss of electrons by a substance in a chemical reaction.

. . . .

PARAGRAPH

. . . .

PARALLEL

. . . .

PARALLEL CIRCUIT

A group of sentences about the same idea.

. . . .

Lines in the same plane that will never intersect.

Definition	Example
two lines on a flat surface (also called a plane in geometry) that never intersect (the symbol ‖ indicates that two lines are parallel)	A <———————————> B <———————————> A ‖ B

. . . .

A circuit with more than one path for an electrical current to follow.

PARALLEL STRUCTURE

. . . .

Two or more equivalent ideas in a sentence that have the same purpose, presented in the same form.

Example:

Not parallel: *We came, we saw, and it was conquered by us.*

(The first two clauses use the active *we + past tense verb* construction; the third uses a passive structure with a prepositional phrase.)

Parallel: *We came, we saw, we conquered.*

(All three clauses start with *we* and use a past tense verb.)

· ·

PARALLELOGRAM

. . . .

P

A quadrilateral with two pairs of parallel sides.

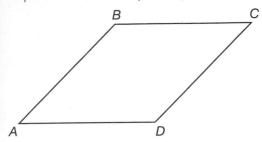

In this figure, line $AB \parallel CD$ and $BC \parallel AD$.

A parallelogram has:

- opposite sides that are equal ($AB = CD$ and $BC = AD$)
- opposite angles that are equal ($m\angle a = m\angle c$ and $m\angle b = m\angle d$)
- and consecutive angles that are supplementary ($m\angle a + m\angle b = 180°$, $m\angle b + m\angle c = 180°$, $m\angle c + m\angle d = 180°$, $m\angle d + m\angle a = 180°$)

PARENTHESES

. . . .

PARLIAMENT

. . . .

**PAST PERFECT PROGRESSIVE
TENSE**

Symbols ( ) used to enclose explanatory material that interrupts the normal flow of a sentence. They also enclose information when accuracy is essential and enclose letters or numbers in a list, marking a division from the rest of the text.

. . . .

A national legislative body made up of elected and sometimes non-elected officials. The British Parliament is made up of the House of Commons and the House of Lords.

. . . .

Verb form that shows continuing action that began in the past. For example, "She *had been painting* the door before the cat scratched it."

PAST PERFECT TENSE

. . . .

PAST PROGRESSIVE TENSE

. . . .

PAST TENSE

P

Verb form that shows an action completed in the past or completed before some other past action. For example, "Kristen *had never been* to an opera before last night."

. . . .

Verb form that shows a continuing action in the past. For example, "We *were eating* dinner when the phone rang."

. . . .

Verb form that shows action that happened in the past. For example, "He *washed* his car."

PEARL HARBOR

. . . .

PEMDAS

. . . .

A United States military base in the Pacific Ocean that was attacked by Japan in 1941. The attack led to the entry of the United States into World War II.

· ·

An order for doing a sequence of mathematical operations (see *order of operations*):

P (Parentheses): Perform all operations within parentheses first.

E (Exponents): Evaluate exponents.

M (Multiply): Work from left to right in your expression.

D (Divide): Work from left to right in your expression.

A (Add): Work from left to right in your expression.

S (Subtract): Work from left to right in your expression.

Example:

$$\frac{(5 + 3)^2}{4} + 27 =$$

$$\frac{(8)^2}{4} + 27 =$$

$$\frac{64}{4} + 27 =$$

$$16 + 27 = \mathbf{43}$$

· ·

PENTAGON

. . . .

P

A polygon with five sides.

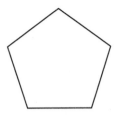

· ·

PERCENT

P

A ratio or fraction whose denominator is assumed to be 100, expressed using the % sign; 98% is equal to $\frac{98}{100}$.

Percent	Decimal	Fraction
1%	0.01	$\frac{1}{100}$
5%	0.05	$\frac{5}{100}$
10%	0.10	$\frac{1}{10}$
12.5%	0.125	$\frac{1}{8}$
20%	0.20	$\frac{1}{5}$
25%	0.25	$\frac{1}{4}$
$33\frac{1}{3}\%$	0.33 (rounded)	$\frac{1}{3}$
40%	0.40	$\frac{2}{5}$
50%	0.50	$\frac{1}{2}$
$66\frac{2}{3}\%$	0.67 (rounded)	$\frac{2}{3}$
75%	0.75	$\frac{3}{4}$
80%	0.80	$\frac{4}{5}$
90%	0.90	$\frac{9}{10}$
100%	1.00	$\frac{1}{1} = 1$

PERIMETER

. . . .

PERIOD

. . . .

PERPENDICULAR

The distance around the outside of a polygon.
Formulas for finding the perimeter of:
- Square: $P = 4 \times S$, where S is the length of any one side
- Rectangle: $P = 2 \times \text{length} + 2 \times \text{width}$
- Triangle: $P = \text{side}_1 + \text{side}_2 + \text{side}_3$

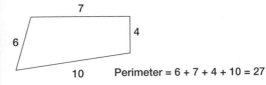

Perimeter = 6 + 7 + 4 + 10 = 27

• •

The time, often measured in seconds, for one complete repetition or rotation.

• •

Two lines that intersect to form 90° angles.

$A \perp B$

(the symbol $\perp$ indicates that two lines are perpendicular).

PERSONIFICATION

. . . .

PHLOEM

. . . .

PHOTON

Figurative language that endows non-human
or non-animal objects with human characteristics. For example, "The candle flame danced
in the dark." A candle flame cannot actually
dance; this is a different way to describe that
the flame flickered.

. . . .

Vascular tissue found in plants that transports
mostly sugar and water; can travel either
"shoot to root" or "root to shoot."

. . . .

A particle of light. A discreet amount of light
energy where a single photon of light is the
smallest unit of light energy possible.

PHOTOSYNTHESIS

. . . .

PHYSICAL PROPERTY

. . . .

PILGRIMS

A process by which the sunlight's energy, water, and carbon dioxide are transformed into sugar and oxygen.

$$6CO_2 + 6H_2O \rightarrow C_6H_{12}O_6 + 6O_2$$

. . . .

A property that can be observed without performing a chemical transformation of that substance.

. . . .

A group of religious separatists who were the founders of the Plymouth Colony on the coast of Massachusetts in 1620.

PLATE TECTONICS

. . . .

PLOT

. . . .

PLURALITY SYSTEM

P

The theory in which Earth's crust is made up of many plates that float on the mantle. This theory explains the movement of the continents, the formation of mountains, earthquakes, volcanoes, and the existence of mid-oceanic ridges.

· ·

The ordering of events in a story.

· ·

An electoral system in which a candidate need only receive more votes than his or her opponent to win.

PLYMOUTH COLONY

. . . .

POETRY

. . . .

POINT

P

A settlement made by Pilgrims on the coast of Massachusetts in 1620.

∙ ∙

Literature written in verse.

∙ ∙

A location in space.

POINT OF VIEW

. . . .

POLAR ZONE

. . . .

POLITICAL PARTY

P

The perspective from which something is told or written.

. . . .

The climatic zone near the North and South Poles characterized by long, cold winters and short, cool summers.

. . . .

An organization that presents its positions on public issues and promotes candidates that support its point of view. Political parties serve several functions:
- recruit candidates and run election campaigns
- formulate positions on issues that affect the public and propose solutions
- educate the public on issues
- mobilize their members to vote
- create voting blocs in Congress

POLYGON

. . . .

POLYMER

. . . .

A closed two-dimensional shape made up of several line segments that are joined together.

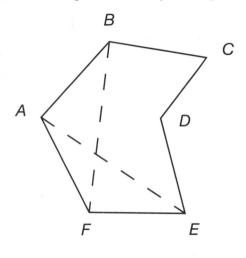

. . . .

A large molecule made up of repeating units of one or more small molecules (monomers).

. . . .

POLYNOMIAL

. . . .

POLYTHEISTIC

. . . .

P

A number, variable, or combination of a number and a variable.

- A **monomial** is a polynomial with one term, as in $2b^3$.
- A **binomial** is a polynomial with two unlike terms, as in $5x + 3y$.
- A **trinomial** is a polynomial with three unlike terms, as in $y^2 + 2z - 6$.

• •

The worship or belief in many Gods. Polytheistic religious systems include Buddhism, Hinduism, and Shintoism.

Religion	Origin	Characteristics
Hinduism	India in 1500 B.C.	• Hinduism has no single founder; it developed over a period of 4,000 years. • One of its main features is a caste system, in which people are born into a prescribed class and follow the ways of that class.
Buddhism	India in 525 B.C.	• It was founded by Siddhartha Gautama, called the Buddha. • Buddhists believe in a cycle of rebirth. • The ultimate goal of the Buddhist path is to achieve nirvana, an enlightened state free from suffering.

• •

POPULATION

. . . .

POSITION

. . . .

POSITIVE NUMBER

The size, makeup, and distribution of people in a given area.

• •

The location of an object in a coordinate system. Common units of measure are meters (m).

• •

A real number whose value is greater than zero.

POSSESSIVE CASE PRONOUNS

. . . .

POTENTIAL DIFFERENCE

. . . .

P

Pronouns that show ownership, such as *my*, *our*, *your*, *his*, *her*, *their*, *its*.

Possessive Pronoun	Meaning	Example
its	belonging to it	*The dog chased its tail.*
your	belonging to you	*Your time is up.*
their	belonging to them	*Their words were comforting.*
whose	belonging to who	*Whose tickets are these?*

• •

The difference in electric potential energy per unit charge between two points. This is commonly called *voltage*. The common unit of measure for potential difference is volts (V).

• •

POTENTIAL ENERGY

. . . .

PRECESSION

. . . .

PRECISION

P

The energy due to an object's position or state.

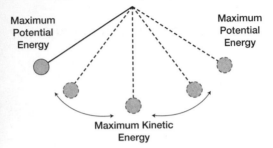

Maximum Potential Energy

Maximum Potential Energy

Maximum Kinetic Energy

The change of potential energy into kinetic energy, and kinetic energy into potential energy, in a pendulum.

· ·

The process by which Earth's axis traces out a circle on the celestial sphere.

· ·

The measurement of the closeness of measurements obtained from two or more experimental runs.

PRESENT PERFECT PROGRESSIVE TENSE

. . . .

PRESENT PERFECT TENSE

. . . .

PRESENT PROGRESSIVE TENSE

P

Verb form that shows action that began in the past and is continuing in the present. For example, "They *have been talking* for the last hour."

• •

Verb form that shows an action that began in the past. For example, "I *have seen* that movie ten times."

• •

Verb form that shows an action happening now, and ends in the suffix *–ing*. For example, "They *are sleeping*."

PRESENT TENSE

. . . .

PRESSURE

. . . .

PRIMARY ELECTION

Verb form that shows action that happens now or action that happens routinely. For example, "I *run* in the park."

. . . .

Force per unit area. Units used to measure pressure are torr, atmosphere (atm), and pascal (Pa). $p = \frac{F}{A}$

. . . .

A preliminary contest in which voters give their preference for a political party's candidate for public office.

PRIME MERIDIAN

. . . .

PRIME NUMBER

. . . .

PROCEDURE

An imaginary line that runs north and south through Greenwich, England at 0° longitude.

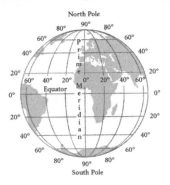

North Pole

Prime Meridian

Equator

South Pole

. . . .

A real number that is divisible by only two positive factors: 1 and itself. For example, 5 is a prime number, as only 1 and 5 divide it.

. . . .

A logical list of steps that explain the exact actions taken to perform an experiment.

PRODUCT

. . . .

PROGRESSIVISM

. . . .

PROJECTILE

P

The result when two numbers are multiplied together. For example, the product of 4 × 3 is 12.

These words . . .	**. . . often translate into these math symbols**
multiplied by product times	×, · ( ) Parentheses can also indicate multiplication. 3(5) is the same as 3 × 5 or 3 · 5.

. . . .

A reform movement of the early twentieth century that sought to remedy the problems created by industrialization.

. . . .

An object in two-dimensional motion that has a vertical acceleration equal to –g (or g down-ward) and a horizontal acceleration of zero.

PRONOUN

. . . .

PROPER FRACTION

. . . .

PROPER NOUNS

P

A word used in place of a noun; includes *I*, *my*, *she*, *he*, *them*, *theirs*, *it*.

	Singular	**Plural**
First person	I, me	we, us, our
Second person	you	you (all)
Third person	he, she, it, one	they, them, their

· ·

A fraction whose denominator is larger than its numerator. Proper fractions are equal to or less than 1. (e.g., $\frac{3}{5}$, $\frac{7}{8}$, etc.)

· ·

Nouns that name a specific person, place, or thing. Proper nouns must be capitalized. Some examples of proper nouns include days of the week, holidays, historical events, names of people, landmarks, cities and states, names of products, and works of art and literature.

PROPORTION

. . . .

PROPORTIONAL REPRESENTATION

. . . .

PROSE

A relationship between two equivalent sets of fractions in the form $ab = cd$. For example, $\frac{2}{3} = \frac{6}{9}$.

Example:

$\frac{8}{10} = \frac{?}{100}$

Divide the denominator into the new denominator, which is 100: $100 \div 10 = 10$.

Multiply 10 by the numerator: $8 \times 10 = 80$.

Write 80 over the new denominator: $\frac{80}{100}$.

. . . .

An electoral process in which political parties are awarded a proportion of legislative seats based on the percentage of votes they received.

. . . .

Literature that is not written in verse or dramatic form.

PROTAGONIST

. . . .

PROTEIN SYNTHESIS

. . . .

PUN

P

The "hero" or main character of a story that faces the central conflict.

· ·

A process by which DNA will transport its information by way of RNA to the ribosomes where proteins will be assembled.

· ·

A play on the meaning of a word.

P

PURITANS

. . . .

PYTHAGOREAN THEOREM

. . . .

A group of English migrants who sought to purify the Church of England. The group started settlements in New England in the seventeenth century.

• •

Theorem stating that in all right triangles, the sum of the squares of the two legs is equal to the square of the hypotenuse: $\text{leg}^2 + \text{leg}^2 = \text{hypotenuse}^2$. Another different way to state this is: $a^2 + b^2 = c^2$, where a and b are the legs and c is the hypotenuse of the right triangle.

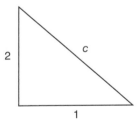

$a^2 + b^2 = c^2$
$1^2 + 2^2 = c^2$
$1 + 4 = c^2$
$5 = c^2$
$\sqrt{5} = c$

• •

QUADRANTS

. . . .

The four equal parts of a coordinate plane.
A number names each quadrant. The upper-
right-hand area is quadrant I. You proceed
counterclockwise to name the other quadrants.

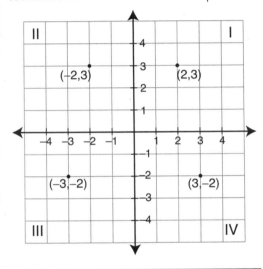

Points	Sign of Coordinates	Quadrant
(2,3)	(+,+)	I
(−2,3)	(−,+)	II
(−3,−2)	(−,−)	III
(3,−2)	(+,−)	IV

. . . .

QUADRILATERAL

. . . .

QUALITATIVE OBSERVATION

. . . .

QUANTITATIVE OBSERVATION

A polygon with four sides.

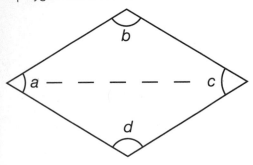

. . . .

An observation that includes characteristics other than amounts or measurements; may include shapes, colors, actions, and odors.

. . . .

An observation that includes characteristics of measurements or amounts.

QUATRAIN

. . . .

QUOTATION MARKS

. . . .

QUOTIENT

In poetry, a stanza of four lines.

. . . .

Symbols (" ") used to set off a direct quotation or thought within a sentence or paragraph. They are also used to set off unfamiliar terms and nicknames. Do not use quotation marks for paraphrases or indirect quotations.

. . . .

The result when one number is divided into another. For example, when dividing 6 by 3, the quotient is 2.

These words . . .	. . . often translate into these math symbols
divided by quotient per	÷, /

RADIATION

. . . .

RADICAL

. . . .

RADICAND

The emission of energy.

. . . .

The symbol used to signify a root operation.
($\sqrt{}$)

. . . .

The number or mathematical expression inside of a radical. For example, 12 is the radicand in $\sqrt{12}$.

RADIUS

. . . .

RATE

. . . .

RATIFY

Any line segment from the center of a circle to a point on the curve of the circle. The radius of a circle is equal to half the diameter.

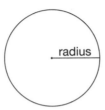

· ·

A ratio comparing two items with unlike units. Some common rates include the following:

calories per serving	feet per yard
cents per pound	heartbeats per minute
dollars per hour	inches per foot
dollars per pound	miles per gallon
dollars per year	miles per hour
feet per mile	words per minute

· ·

To confirm or give formal approval to something, such as an agreement between nations.

RATIO

. . . .

RAY

. . . .

REACTANT

The relationship between two things, expressed as a proportion. Here are some examples of ways to write ratios:

- with the word *to*: 1 to 2
- using a colon (:) to separate the numbers: 1:2
- using the phrase *for every*: 1 for every 2
- separated by a division sign or fraction bar: 1/2 or $\frac{1}{2}$

· ·

A line which includes a clearly defined starting point, but has no end point.

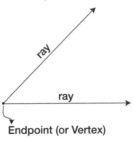

Endpoint (or Vertex)

· ·

A substance that is consumed in a chemical reaction to form products.

READABILITY

. . . .

REAL NUMBERS

. . . .

RECESSION

R

Techniques and strategies that writers use to make information easier to process, including the use of headings and lists.

. . . .

Numbers that include fractions and decimals in addition to integers (e.g., –1, 0, 1, $\frac{3}{4}$, 0.125, $\sqrt{12}$, etc.).

. . . .

A period of low economic productivity and income.

RECIPROCAL

. . . .

RECONSTRUCTION

. . . .

RECTANGLE

One of two numbers that, when multiplied together, give a product of 1. For instance, since $\frac{3}{2} \times \frac{2}{3}$ is equal to 1, $\frac{3}{2}$ is the reciprocal of $\frac{2}{3}$.

• •

From 1865 to 1877, the period of readjustment and rebuilding of the South that followed the American Civil War.

• •

A parallelogram with four right angles.

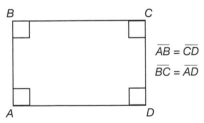

$$\overline{AB} = \overline{CD}$$
$$\overline{BC} = \overline{AD}$$

REDUCTION

. . . .

REDUNDANCY

. . . .

REFLEXIVE PRONOUN

R

The gain of electrons by a substance in a chemical reaction.

. . . .

The same idea expressed twice using different words; words with meanings that overlap.

→ The use of unnecessary words or phrases

   Redundant: Turn left at the <u>green-colored</u> house.

   Correct: Turn left at the <u>green</u> house.

→ Unnecessary repetition of nouns or pronouns

   Redundant: <u>Riva she</u> couldn't believe her ears.

   Correct: <u>Riva</u> couldn't believe her ears.

. . . .

A pronoun that includes the word *self* or *selves*: *myself, yourself, himself, herself, ourselves, themselves.*

REGION

. . . .

REMAINDER

. . . .

RENAISSANCE

A land area that shares cultural, political, or geographic attributes that distinguish it from other areas.

. . . .

The amount left over after a division problem using whole numbers. For example, $\frac{55}{7}$ = 7, with a remainder of 6. Divisible numbers always have a remainder of zero.

. . . .

A term meaning "rebirth" that refers to a series of cultural and literary developments in Europe in the fourteenth, fifteenth, and sixteenth centuries.

RENEWABLE RESOURCE

. . . .

REPEAL

. . . .

REPUBLIC

R

A renewable resource is replaced in nature as quickly as it is used. Plants and crops are examples of resources that are replenishable.

. . . .

To take back or undo, typically referring to the repeal of an amendment to the U.S. Constitution.

. . . .

A government based on the concept that power resides with the people, who then elect officials to represent them in government.

RESERVE RATIO

....

RESISTANCE

....

RESPIRATION

A portion of deposits that banks, which are members of the Federal Reserve system, set aside and do not use to make loans.

. . . .

The resistance to the flow of electrons through a circuit. The resistance is dependent on the current flowing through the circuit element and the voltage across the circuit element; resistance is measured in ohms (Ω).

$$R = \frac{V}{I}$$

. . . .

A process by which sugar is converted into ATP and carbon dioxide; may include oxygen, which is called *aerobic respiration*.

$$C_6H_{12}O_6 + 6O_2 \rightarrow 6CO_2 + 6H_2O$$

RESTRICTIVE CLAUSE

. . . .

RETROGRADE MOTION

. . . .

REVERSIBLE REACTION

Group of words that, if omitted from a sentence, changes the entire meaning of the sentence, or even makes the sentence untrue. The restrictive clause is not set off with commas. Also known as an *essential clause*.

· ·

The apparent westward motion of objects in the sky from one night to another.

· ·

A reaction in which products can revert back into reactants.

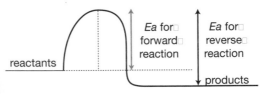

The activation energies (*Ea*) for the forward reaction (reactants forming products) and for the reverse reaction (products forming reactants) are about the same. Such a reaction is reversible.

REVOLUTION

. . . .

RHOMBUS

. . . .

RHYME

A violent change in the political order and social structure of a society.

．．．．．．．．．．．．．．．．．．．．．．．．．

A parallelogram with four equal and congruent sides.

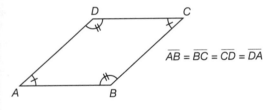

$$\overline{AB} = \overline{BC} = \overline{CD} = \overline{DA}$$

．．．．．．．．．．．．．．．．．．．．．．．．．

The repetition of an identical or similar stressed sound(s) at the end of words.

RHYTHM

....

RIBOSOME

....

The overall sound or "musical" effect of the pattern of words and sentences.

· ·

An organelle where protein synthesis occurs. Ribosomes can be found floating freely in the cytoplasm or attached to the outside of endoplasmic reticulum.

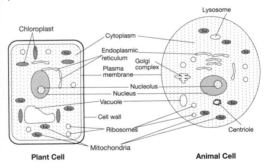

Plant Cell   Animal Cell

· ·

RIGHT ANGLE

. . . .

RIGHT ASCENSION

. . . .

An angle that measures exactly 90°.

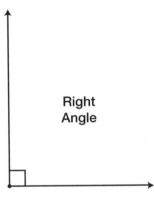

Right Angle

. . . .

The celestial coordinate similar to that of longitude on Earth. Right ascension is measured in hours, minutes, and seconds, with 24 hours making up 360° around the celestial sphere.

. . . .

RIGHT TRIANGLE

. . . .

RIVER SYSTEMS

. . . .

A triangle with a right angle. In a right triangle, the side opposite the right angle is called the hypotenuse. This will be the longest side of the right triangle.

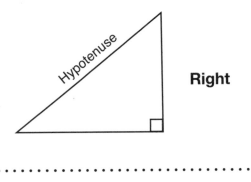

Right

· ·

A river and its associated tributaries and drainage basin.

· ·

RNA

· ·

ROCK CYCLE

· ·

ROMANOV DYNASTY

R

Abbreviation for ribonucleic acid. RNA is responsible for transmitting genetic information from the DNA to the ribosomes for protein synthesis.

. . . .

A concept in geology that summarizes how rocks of different types are formed and how they can be transformed from one type into another.

. . . .

The family that ruled Russia from 1613 until the Russian Revolution in 1917.

ROOT

. . . .

ROUNDING

. . . .

One of two (or more) equal factors of a number. The square root of 36 is 6 because $6 \times 6 = 36$. The cube root of 27 is 3 because $3 \times 3 \times 3 = 27$.

. . . .

Reducing the digits in a number while trying to keep its value similar. A rounded number has approximately the same value as the number you start with and is easier to use, but it is less exact.

The general rule for rounding:
- If the number you are rounding is followed by 5, 6, 7, 8, or 9, round the number up. For example, 58 rounded to the nearest ten is 60.
- If the number you are rounding is followed by 0, 1, 2, 3, or 4, round the number down. For example: 53 rounded to the nearest ten is 50.

To the Nearest . . .	Ten	Hundred	Thousand
27,239 rounds to	27,240	27,200	27,000
691 rounds to	690	700	1,000
38 rounds to	40	0	0

. . . .

RULE OF LAW

. . . .

RUN-ON SENTENCE

. . . .

The principle that all citizens, including func-
tionaries of the government, must follow the
law.

• •

A sentence in which independent clauses have
been run together without punctuation (a
period, semicolon, or comma).

Run-on:	The debate is over, now it is time to vote.
Period:	The debate is over. Now it is time to vote.
Comma + conjunction:	The debate is over, and now it is time to vote.
Semicolon:	The debate is over; now it is time to vote.
Dash:	The debate is over—now it is time to vote.
Subordinating conjunction:	Since the debate is over, it is time to vote.

• •

GED® TEST FLASH REVIEW

SARCASM

. . . .

SATIRE

. . . .

SCALAR

Sharp, biting language intended to ridicule its subject.

. . . .

A form of writing that exposes and ridicules its subject with the hope of bringing about change.

. . . .

A quantity that has a magnitude or amount only.

SCALE

. . . .

A special ratio used for models of real-life items.

On scale drawings, the scale will be a comparison of a small distance unit, like inches, to a large distance unit, like feet or even miles. So a scale on a map could read "3 inches = 10 miles." This means for every 3 inches on the map, the actual distance is 10 miles. This ratio is $\frac{3}{10}$, but care should be taken to remember that the units do not agree. If a scale drawing reads "1 inch = 10 feet," this does not mean that the real item is only 10 times bigger, even though the ratio would be 1:10. Solve scale drawing problems as you would any type of ratio problem, keeping the units consistent and clear in your answer.

Example:

A model locomotive measures 8.7 inches in length. If the scale given is 1:16, how long is the real locomotive?

Because the real train engine is 16 times as big as the model, the real train engine will be 8.7 times 16, which is 139.2 inches, or 11.6 feet.

. . . .

SCIENTIFIC METHOD

. . . .

SCIENTIFIC NOTATION

. . . .

A process by which data is collected to answer an integral question. The major steps are problem, research, hypothesis, procedure, observations and data collection, analysis of data, and conclusion.

. . . .

A special notation used as shorthand for large numbers. Scientific Notation is based on the base number 10 to the e power. The number 123,000,000,000 in scientific notation is written as 1.23×10^{11}.

Example:

What is 23,419 in scientific notation?

Position the decimal point so that there is only one non-zero digit to its left: 2.3419

Count the number of positions you had to move the decimal point to the left, and that will be e: 4.

In scientific notation, 23,419 is written as 2.3419×10^4.

. . . .

SEA BREEZE

. . . .

SECTIONALISM

. . . .

SEDIMENTARY ROCK

The breeze that develops on the shoreline due to unequal heating of the air above the land and ocean. Sea breeze occurs during the day when the air above the ocean is cooler and the air above the land is warmer. The breeze blows from the sea to the land.

．．．．．．．．．．．．．．．．．．．．．．．．．．．．．

The attitude or actions of a region or section of a nation when it supports its own interests over that of the nation as a whole.

．．．．．．．．．．．．．．．．．．．．．．．．．．．．．

A rock made up of sediments that have been deposited, compacted, and cemented over time.

SEMICOLON

....

SENTENCE FRAGMENT

....

Symbol (;) used to separate independent
clauses. This includes independent clauses
that are joined without a conjunction, independent clauses that contain commas even if
the clauses are joined by a conjunction, and
independent clauses connected with a conjunctive adverb.

. . . .

An incomplete sentence segment that is
lacking either a subject or a predicate. Also
called an *incomplete sentence*. To correct a
fragment, add the missing subject or verb or
otherwise change the sentence to complete
the thought.

<u>Incomplete</u>:	Which is simply not true. [No subject. (*Which* is not a subject.)]
<u>Complete</u>:	*That* is simply not true.
<u>Incomplete</u>:	For example, the French Revolution. [No verb.]
<u>Complete</u>:	*The best example is* the French Revolution.

. . . .

SEPARATION OF POWERS

. . . .

SERIES CIRCUIT

. . . .

SETTING

The practice of dividing the authority of a government between different branches to avoid an abuse of power.

· ·

A circuit with only one path for an electrical current to follow. The current in each element in a series circuit is the same.

· ·

The time and place in which a story unfolds.

SHORTAGE

. . . .

SIGNED NUMBER

. . . .

SIMILE

When demand for a good or service is greater
than that which is produced.

. . . .

A number with a positive or negative sign in
front of it.

. . . .

A type of figurative language that compares
two things using *like* or *as*. For example, the
expression "as blind *as* a bat" indicates that
the person cannot see any better than a bat
can.

SIMPLE INTEREST FORMULA

. . . .

SIMPLIFY TERMS

. . . .

SITUATIONAL IRONY

Interest = principal × rate × time

Example:

To calculate the interest on $1,000.00 at 5% interest per year after 5 year(s):
- *P* is the principal amount or loan amount: $1,000.00
- *r* is the interest rate: 5% per year, which in decimal form is $\frac{5}{100} = 0.05$
- *t* is 5 year(s)

To find the interest, multiply $1,000.00 × 0.05 × 5. The interest payable is: $250.00.

· ·

To combine like terms and reduce an equation to its most basic form.

· ·

The tone that results when there is incongruity between what is expected to happen and what actually occurs.

SLOPE

. . . .

SLOPE-INTERCEPT FORM

. . . .

The steepness of a line. Slope is the rise or decline over the run, or the change in y over the change in x.

· ·

$y = mx + b$. m = slope of the line and b = the y-intercept. The slope-intercept form is also known as "$y =$ form."

· ·

SLOPE OF A LINE ON A COORDINATE PLANE

. . . .

SOCIAL STUDIES

. . . .

Slope of a line: $m = \frac{y_2 - y_1}{x_2 - x_1}$. (x_1, y_1) and (x_2, y_2) are two points on the line.

Example:

Find the slope of a line containing the points (3,2) and (8,9).

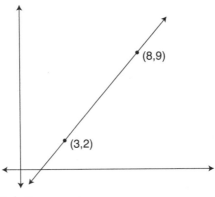

Solution

$\frac{(9-2)}{(8-3)} = \frac{7}{5}$

Therefore, the slope of the line is $\frac{7}{5}$.

. . . .

The study of how people live every day, including the exploration of humans' physical environments, cultures, political institutions, and economic conditions.

. . . .

SOCIALISM

. . . .

SOLILOQUY

. . . .

SOLUBILITY

An economic system in which the state owns and controls the basic factors of production and distribution of wealth.

Characteristics	Examples
• State owns and operates many businesses and services. • Private ownership is allowed. • Citizens pay high taxes to fund state-run social services, including healthcare, food, and housing.	• No current examples, though many EU countries have socialist aspects.

. . . .

In drama, a speech made by a character who reveals his or her thoughts to the audience as if he or she is alone and thinking aloud.

. . . .

The amount of solute that can be dissolved completely in a solvent at a given temperature.

SOLUTION

....

SONNET

....

SPEAKER

A homogeneous mixture of a solute (usually solid, but sometimes liquid or gas) in a solvent (usually a liquid, but sometimes a solid or gas).

· ·

A poem composed of 14 lines, usually in iambic pentameter, with a specific rhyme scheme.

· ·

In poetry, the voice or narrator of the poem.

SPEED

. . . .

SPEED OF LIGHT

. . . .

SPINDLE FIBER

The magnitude of velocity. Speed measures the rate that position changes with time without regard to the direction of motion. Common units are meters per second (m/s).

. . . .

The speed of light in a vacuum is the fastest known speed. As light travels in other materials, it will change speed. The speed of light in any material is still the fastest speed possible in that material. Commonly denoted by the symbol c.

. . . .

An organelle used during mitosis and meiosis that separates and "pulls" chromosomes toward the opposite poles of the cell.

SPONTANEOUS REACTION

. . . .

SQUARE

. . . .

A reaction that does not require an external source of energy to proceed.

· ·

A parallelogram with both four equal and right angles and four congruent sides. A square, a parallelogram, a rhombus, and a rectangle share the same properties: opposite sides are parallel and congruent, opposite angles are congruent, consecutive angles are supplementary, and diagonals bisect each other.

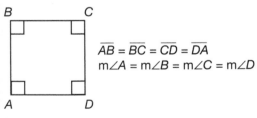

$$\overline{AB} = \overline{BC} = \overline{CD} = \overline{DA}$$
$$m\angle A = m\angle B = m\angle C = m\angle D$$

· ·

STAGE DIRECTIONS

. . . .

STAMP ACT

. . . .

In drama, the instructions provided by the playwright that explain how the action should be staged, including directions for props, costumes, lighting, tone, and character movements.

. . . .

A measure passed by the British Parliament in 1765 as a means of collecting taxes in the American colonies. It required that all printed materials, including legal documents and newspapers, carry a tax stamp.

. . . .

STANZA

. . . .

STAR

. . . .

A group of lines in a poem; a poetic paragraph.

Example:
A Poison Tree

(1) I was angry with my friend:
    I told my wrath, my wrath did end.
    I was angry with my foe;
    I told it not, my wrath did grow. } stanza 1

(5) And I water'd it in fears,
    Night & morning with my tears;
    And I sunned it with smiles,
    And with soft deceitful wiles. } stanza 2

    And it grew both by day and night,
(10) Till it bore an apple bright.
    And my foe beheld it shine,
    And he knew that it was mine. } stanza 3

    And into my garden stole
    When the night had veil'd the pole;
(15) In the morning glad I see
    My foe outstretch'd beneath the tree. } stanza 4

. . . .

A body composed mostly of hydrogen and helium that radiates energy and that has fusion actively occurring in the core.

. . . .

STATES OF MATTER

. . . .

STOCK EXCHANGE

. . . .

Solid, liquid, and gas. In solids, atoms or
molecules are held in place. The shape and
volume of a solid usually do not vary much.
In liquids, atoms or molecules can move, but
their motion is constrained by other molecules.
Liquids assume the shape of their container.
In gases, the motion of atoms or molecules is
unrestricted. Gases assume both the volume
and the shape of their containers and they are
easily compressible.

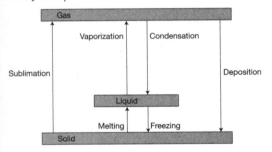

Phase changes between the three states of
matter.

· ·

An organized market for buying and selling
stocks and bonds.

· ·

STOCK MARKET CRASH OF 1929

. . . .

STRAIGHT ANGLE

. . . .

STRUCTURE

S

A collapse in the value of stocks that marked the onset of the Great Depression in the United States.

. . . .

An angle that measures 180°.

Straight Angle
180°

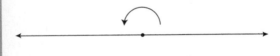

. . . .

The manner in which a work of literature is organized; its order of arrangement and divisions.

STYLE

. . . .

SUB-GENRE

. . . .

SUBJECT

The manner in which a text is written, composed of word choice, sentence structure, and level of formality and detail.

. . . .

A category within a larger category.

. . . .

Someone or something that performs the action or serves as the main focus of a sentence.

The subject of a sentence can be **singular** or **compound** (plural):

I slept all day.
singular
subject

Kendrick and I worked all night.
compound subject (two subjects performing the action)

SUBJECT-VERB AGREEMENT

. . . .

SUBORDINATE CLAUSE

. . . .

The rule that states that the subject in a clause—the person or thing doing the action—must match the verb in number. For example, if the subject is singular, the verb must be singular; if the subject is plural, the verb must be plural.

<u>Incorrect:</u> *They doesn't have a chance against Coolidge.*
(plural subject, singular verb)

<u>Correct:</u> *They don't have a chance against Coolidge.*
(plural subject, plural verb)

. . . .

A group of words that has both a subject and a verb but (unlike an independent clause) cannot stand alone as a sentence. Also known as a *dependent clause*.

Independent clause: *She was excited.*
Dependent clause: *Because she was excited.*

Notice that the dependent clause is incomplete; it needs an additional thought to make a complete sentence, such as:

<u>She spoke very quickly</u> *because she was excited.*

The independent clause, however, can stand alone. It is a complete thought.

. . . .

SUFFRAGE

. . . .

SUM

. . . .

The right to vote.

. . . .

The result of adding two numbers together. The sum of 5 + 2 is 7.

These words . . .	. . . often translate into these math symbols
added to	+
sum	
plus	
increased by	
combine	
all together	

. . . .

SUPPLEMENTARY ANGLES

. . . .

SUPPLY

. . . .

Two angles are supplementary if the sum of their measures is equal to 180°.

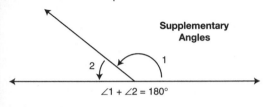

Supplementary Angles

∠1 + ∠2 = 180°

. . . .

The amount of goods and services available for purchase.

. . . .

SURFACE AREA

. . . .

SURPLUS

. . . .

The measurement of the area of each face of an object.

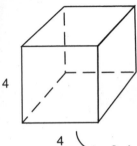

4

4

Surface area of front side = 16
Therefore, the surface area
of the cube = 16 × 6 = 96.

. . . .

When the supply of a good or service is greater than that which customers are willing to buy (demand).

. . . .

SUSPENSE

. . . .

SYMBOL

. . . .

The state of anxiety caused by an undecided or unresolved situation.

· ·

A person, place, or object invested with special meaning to represent something else.

· ·

TARIFF

. . . .

TEMPERANCE ZONE

. . . .

TEMPERATURE

T

A tax on imported, and sometimes exported,
goods.

. . . .

A climatic zone characterized by four seasons:
usually a hot summer, cold winter, and moder-
ate spring and fall.

. . . .

The measure of the average kinetic energy of
the molecules of a substance.

TENSION

....

TERMINAL MORAINE

....

TERRESTRIAL PLANET

The force that acts and is transferred along ropes, strings, and chains.

· ·

A ridge of material deposited by a glacier at its farthest point of advance.

· ·

One of the inner planets of the solar system that have characteristics similar to that of Earth. The terrestrial planets are Mercury, Venus, Earth, and Mars. They are small, have few or no moons, and have no rings. They have a thin or no atmosphere, are rocky, and have high density and low mass. Terrestrial planets are located close to the sun and are close to each other. They have long rotation rates and short revolution periods around the sun.

THEME

. . . .

THESIS

. . . .

THESIS STATEMENT

T

The overall meaning or idea of a literary work.

· ·

The main idea of a nonfiction text.

· ·

The sentence(s) that expresses an author's thesis.

TONE

. . . .

TOPIC SENTENCE

. . . .

A writer's emotional attitude toward the subject or audience. The mood or attitude conveyed by writing or voice.

Here are some common words used to describe tone:

cheerful	hopeful	sad	gloomy
apologetic	critical	sincere	insincere
sarcastic	ironic	playful	demanding
bossy	indifferent	anxious	respectful
disrespectful	foreboding	uncertain	threatening
matter-of-fact	somber	grateful	annoyed
humorous	mocking	defeated	uplifting
timid	joyful	secure	insecure
hesitant	bold	rude	proud
complimentary	angry	confident	mischievous

. . . .

The sentence in a paragraph that expresses the main idea of that paragraph.

. . . .

TOPOGRAPHY

. . . .

TOTAL COST

. . . .

TOTALITARIANISM

The representation of features of land surfaces, including the shape and elevation of terrain, primarily through mapping.

· ·

Total cost = number of units × price per unit

· ·

A government in which the rulers of the state control all aspects of society, including economic, political, cultural, intellectual, and spiritual life.

TOWNSHEND ACTS

. . . .

TRAGEDY

. . . .

TRAGIC FLAW

T

Measures passed by British Parliament in 1767 that taxed American colonists for imported glass, lead, paints, paper, and tea.

· ·

A play that presents a character's fall due to a tragic flaw.

· ·

The characteristic of a hero in a tragedy that causes his or her downfall.

TRAGIC HERO

. . . .

TRAGICOMEDY

. . . .

TRANSPIRATION

T

The character in a tragedy who falls from greatness and accepts responsibility for that fall.

· ·

A tragic play that includes comic scenes.

· ·

Process where plants draw on water from the soil and release it as vapor through pores in their leaves.

TRANSVERSAL

. . . .

TRANSVERSE WAVE

. . . .

A line that cuts across two or more lines in the same plane at different points. When a transversal passes through lines that are parallel, (as is often the case), both congruent and supplementary angles are produced.

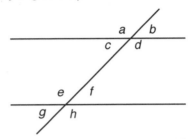

In the previous figure:
- ∠b, ∠c, ∠f, and ∠g are all acute and equal.
- ∠a, ∠d, ∠e, and ∠h are all obtuse and equal.
- Also, any acute angle added to any obtuse angle will be supplementary.

• •

A wave where the motion of the particles in the medium is perpendicular to the direction of wave propagation. Light is an example of a transverse wave.

• •

TRAPEZOID

. . . .

TREATY

. . . .

TREATY OF VERSAILLES

A quadrilateral with one pair of parallel sides.

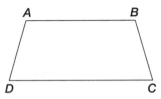

· ·

A formal agreement between sovereign nations or groups of nations.

· ·

The major treaty of five peace treaties that ended World War I in 1919.

TRIANGLE

. . . .

TRINOMIAL

. . . .

TROPIC OF CANCER

A polygon with three sides.

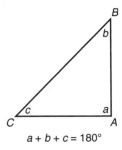

$$a + b + c = 180°$$

· ·

An expression with three terms; for example,
$a + b + c$.

· ·

An imaginary line at 23.5° north latitude.

TROPIC OF CAPRICORN

. . . .

TROPICAL ZONE

. . . .

An imaginary line at 23.5° south latitude.

. . . .

A climatic zone characterized by a hot, wet climate with few seasons.

. . . .

UNDERSTATEMENT

· ·

UNEMPLOYMENT

· ·

UNIFORM CIRCULAR MOTION

A statement that is deliberately restrained.

. . . .

When willing and able wage earners cannot find jobs. The unemployment rate serves as one index of a nation's economic activity.

. . . .

Motion with constant speed in a circle. Since the direction of the velocity changes in this case, there is acceleration even though the speed is constant.

URBANIZATION

. . . .

The movement of a population from rural areas to cities with the result of urban growth.

. . . .

VALENCE

. . . .

VARIABLE

. . . .

Electrons that are in the outer atomic shell and can participate in a chemical reaction.

. . . .

A letter, often x, used to represent an unknown number value in a problem.

Math Relationship: In Words	Translated into an Algebraic Expression
a number plus six	$x + 6$
five times a number	$5x$
three less than a number	$x - 3$
the product of seven and a number	$7x$
a number divided by eight	$x \div 8$ or $\frac{x}{8}$
a number squared	x^2

. . . .

VECTOR

. . . .

VEINS

. . . .

VELOCITY

A quantity that has both a magnitude (an amount) and a direction. In one-dimensional motion, direction can be represented by a positive or negative sign. In two-dimensional motion, the direction is represented as an angle in the coordinate system.

. . . .

In plants, veins are found in the leaves. They are sometimes called the *vascular bundle*, which contains the xylem and phloem. In animals, veins are tube-like tissue that usually transports blood.

. . . .

The rate that a position changes per unit of time and the direction it changes in. Common units are meters per second (m/s).

$$V = \frac{d}{t}$$

VENTRICLES

. . . .

VERB

. . . .

VERBAL IRONY

Chambers found in animal hearts that pump
blood away from the heart.

. . . .

A word or phrase that explains an action, such
as *want, run, take, give,* or a state of being,
such as *am, is, are, was, were, be.*

Examples:

> She **yelled** out the window. (action)
>
> I **am** happy to be here. (state of being)
>
> We **feel** very lucky **to be** alive. (state of
> being)
>
> I **should ask** Winston what he **thinks**. (action)

. . . .

When the intended meaning of a word or
phrase is the opposite of its expressed meaning. For example, "Isn't it as pleasant as a root
canal?" implies that whatever occurred was
not pleasant at all.

VERTEX

. . . .

VETO

. . . .

VOICE

The endpoint where two rays join to form an angle.

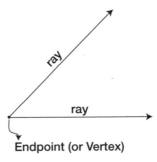

Endpoint (or Vertex)

. . . .

The power of the executive to block the laws passed by the legislative branch.

. . . .

In nonfiction, the sound of the author speaking directly to the reader.

VOLTAGE

....

VOLTMETER

....

See definition for *potential difference*.

· ·

A device used to measure voltage in a circuit.

· ·

VOLUME

V

A cubic measurement that measures how many cubic units it takes to fill a solid figure. Formulas for finding the volume of:

- Cube: $V = s^3$, where s is the length of any edge of the cube
- Rectangular solid: $V = $ length $\times$ width $\times$ height
- Square pyramid: $V = \frac{1}{3} \times$ (base edge)^2 $\times$ height
- Cone: $V = \frac{1}{3} \times \pi \times$ radius^2 $\times$ height; π is approximately equal to 3.14
- Cylinder: $V = \pi \times$ radius^2 $\times$ height; π is approximately equal to 3.14
- Prism: $V = B \times h$ (the area of the base $\times$ the height)

Example:

Find the volume of a cylinder that has a height of 10 cm and a radius of 5 cm.

Choose the correct formula. The problem tells you that you are measuring the volume of a cylinder. The formula for the volume of a cylinder is $V = Ah$ or $V = \pi r^2 h$.

Plug in the known measures and solve:

$$
\begin{aligned}
V &= \pi r^2 h \\
&= \pi(5)^2(10) \\
&= \pi(25)(10) \\
&= \pi(250) \\
&= 785
\end{aligned}
$$

· ·

WATER CYCLE

....

WEIGHT

....

WHOLE NUMBERS

The movement of water between the land, oceans, and atmosphere.

· ·

The force of Earth's gravity on an object. Near the surface of Earth, the weight is equal to the object's mass × the acceleration due to gravity ($W = mg$).

· ·

0, 1, 2, 3, and so on. Whole numbers do not include negatives, fractions, or decimals.

X-AXIS

X

The horizontal line that passes through the origin on a coordinate plane.

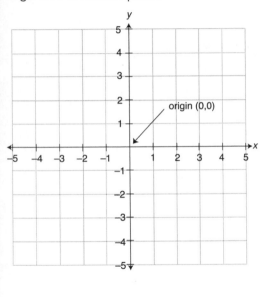

origin (0,0)

. . . .

XYLEM

. . . .

Vascular tissue found in plants that transports water in one direction, from "root to shoot." This is the water that will be sent to the photosynthetic cells in order to perform photosynthesis.

. . . .

Y-AXIS

Y

The vertical line that passes through the origin on a coordinate plane.

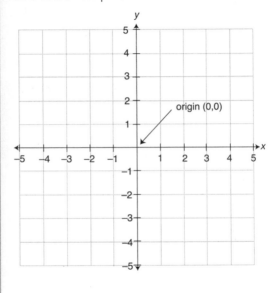

origin (0,0)

. . . .

Y-INTERCEPT

. . . .

YOLK

. . . .

Y

The point where a line graphed on a coordinate plane intersects the *y*-axis.

· ·

The part of an egg that feeds the developing embryo.

· ·

ZOOLOGIST

. . . .

Z

A biologist who studies animal life.

. . . .

NOTES

NOTES

_____

_____

_____

_____

_____

_____

_____

_____

_____

_____

_____

_____

_____

_____

_____

_____

_____

_____

_____

_____

_____

NOTES

NOTES

_____

_____

_____

_____

_____

_____

_____

_____

_____

_____

_____

_____

_____

_____

_____

_____

_____

_____